SEAN·JEF[illegible]LIX[illegible]N

Fairy Paintings

2024

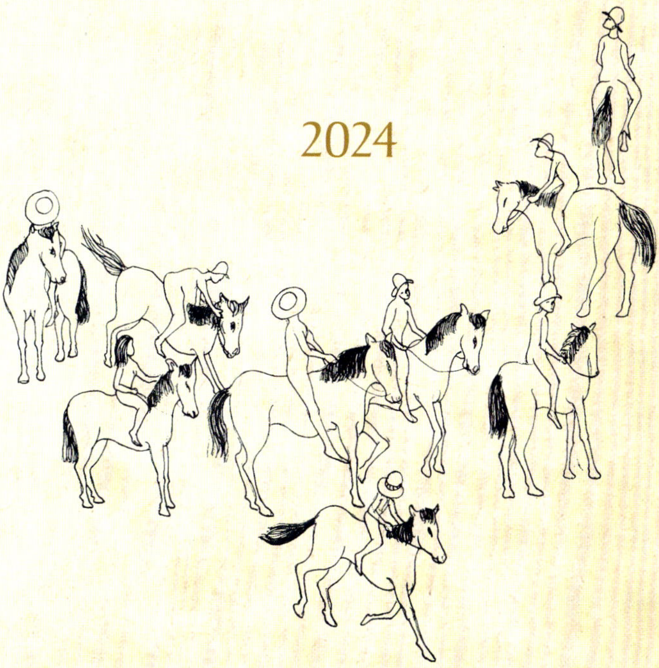

MESSUM'S
DAVID MESSUM FINE ART - EST 1963
www.messums.com
12 Bury Street, St James's, London SW1Y 6AB
+44 (0)20 7287 4448 info@messums.com
davidmessumfineartltd

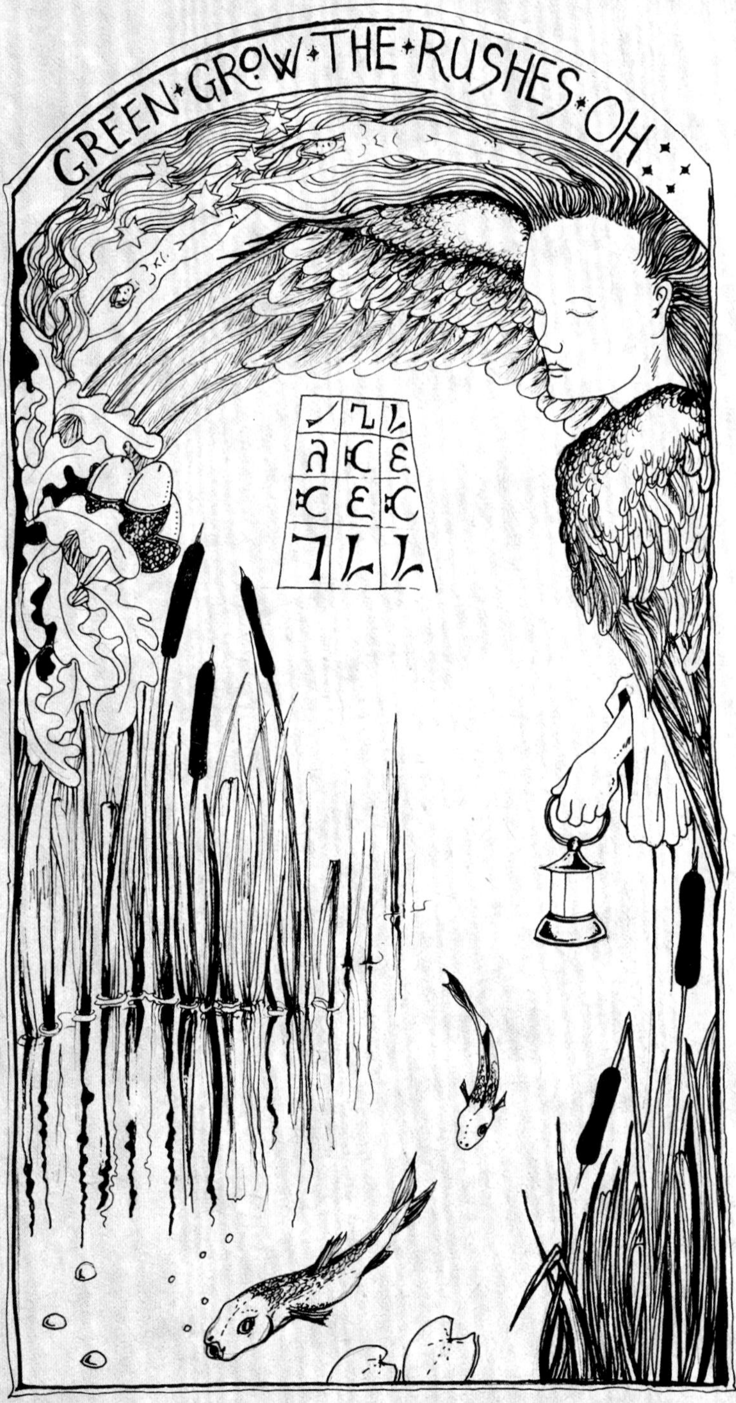
GREEN GROW THE RUSHES OH

Introduction

A Cycle of Paintings Inspired by the Old Folk Song *Green Grow The Rushes Oh*, Often Sung as a Christmas Carol.

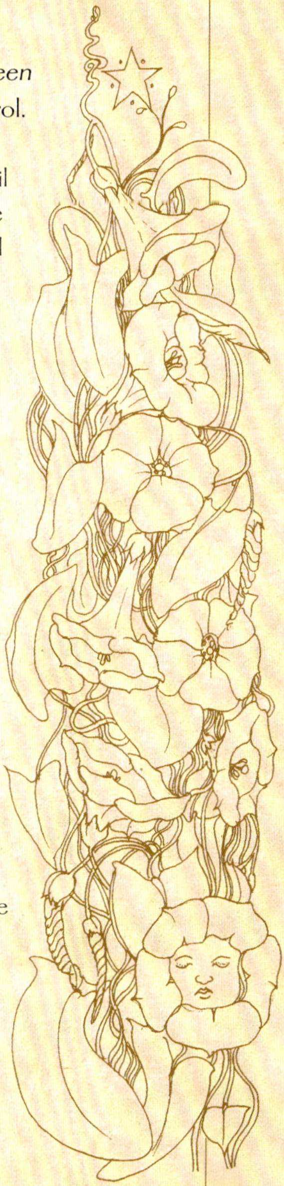

The verses were described by the musicologist Cecil Sharp in 1916 as "so corrupt, indeed, that in some cases we can do little more than guess at their original meaning".

It is generally agreed that the verses mix biblical and astronomical/astrological imagery.

Each painting in the catalogue is accompanied by my rather rambling thoughts regarding the imagery. Artistic or symbolic truth lies only in the visual images themselves which should be seen in this light and not as some academic attempt to find some systematic meaning in what is probably largely nonsense. This should however be qualified as 'serious nonsense' my lifetime study and the wellspring of all my work.

Referring to regular interpretations of the Bible, rushes are first mentioned in Isaiah and symbolise something of no value or impermanence, a theme taken up by Lewis Carroll (see below). The Moses connection with Rushes may be relevant. The name Yahweh (YHVH) is first revealed to Moses and is our One is One and All Alone.... And Ten for Ten Commandments, given to Moses. The 'Green Grow the Rushes O' refrain in the song may be saying something about all the subjects of each verse.

And what exactly is a dream?
And what exactly is a joke?

(from the lyrics of Syd Barrett, central figure in 1960s Psychedelia)

One is One and All Alone and Ever More Shall Be So

From 'le gran' maitre', the almost completely non-interventionist creator god of the most ancient African tradition, through Akhenaten's ill-fated monotheistic worship of The Aten, the solar disc, to YHWH, the highly interventionist God revealed to Moses. Ancient as our song may be it is certainly this last relatively modern iteration of a formless, 'beyond understanding', all powerful deity that is being referred to.

An image of what has become the conventional depiction of Lewis Carroll's *Alice* is perhaps an odd foreground to this painting, but the passage in 'Through the Looking Glass' seems relevant, as Alice pulling up 'the darling scented rushes' then placing them in the bottom of the boat is upset to see them immediately melting away whilst the uncut rushes, further away, remain fresh and more lovely.

Rushes here are a metaphor for the impermanence in anything in human life, in this instance, generally interpreted as Carroll's idyllic state of childhood. This contrasts with the permanent unchanging nature of God.

There may be a Fairie connection as well regarding Carroll, as he gives a good account of the best time to see Fairies in 'Amelia and the Dwarfs' part of 'Sylvie and Bruno' and he was likely aware of William Allingham's poem *The Fairies* which opens with,

Up the airy mountain,
Down the rushy glen,
We daren't go a hunting for fear of little men.
(published in 1850).

A poem we had to recite often at my primary school which always gave me the creeps.

2

One. One is One

oil on board

30 x 20 cms 11 3/4 x 7 7/8 ins

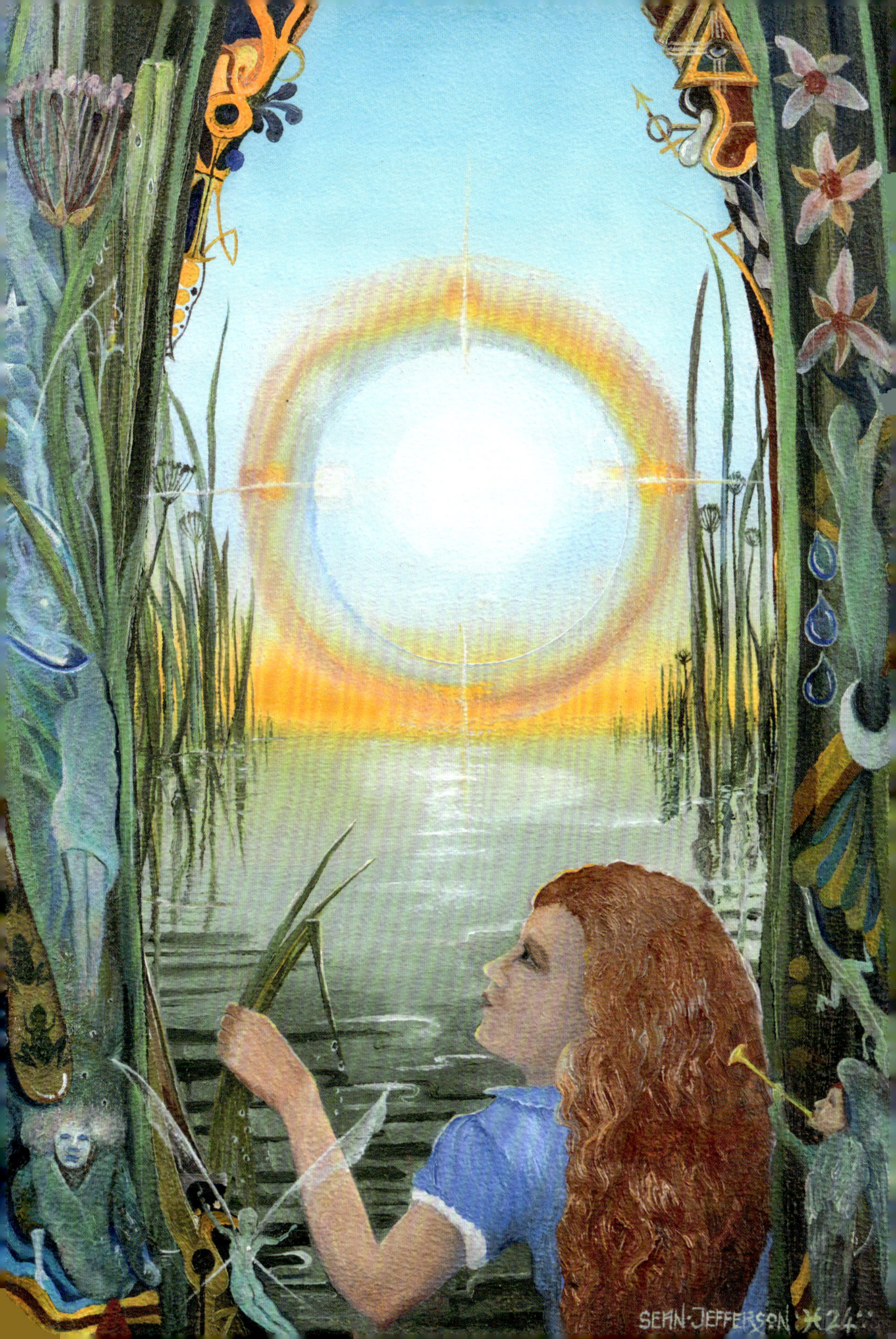
SEAN·JEFFERSON *24

Two, Two the Lilywhite Boys, Dressed all in Green O

In this verse I have taken Robert Graves' interpretation as the basis for the image.

The Lillywhite Boys are representatives of The Oak King and the Holly King who rule the waxing and waning halves of the solar year respectively.

Graves supposes that these characters had physical representatives in deep history, each man being sacrificed to make way for his successor at the winter and summer solstices, memories of this practice leading to a whole range of mythological stories and folk traditions.

This belief system was so entrenched that it was incorporated into early Christianity with John the Baptist and Christ replacing the Old Kings. The carol 'The Holly and The Ivy' being part of this folk memory.

In the Celtic Tree Alphabet the Oak is represented by the equivalent of D in Latin script and the Holly T. Their corresponding months being June 10th to July 7th and July 8th to August 4th respectively. Strangely reeds, a term often interchangeable with rushes, crops up in the alphabet, presumably because of the ubiquitous importance of these plants. The Latin equivalent to the old Celtic being Ng, symbolic of the month October 28th to November 24th.

Graves makes a strong case for these rather impermanent Kings only ruling by permission of The White Goddess. The origins of this belief system being the matriarchal religion, predating patriarchal solar religions.

3

Two. The Lilywhite Boys

oil on board

30 x 20 cms 11 3/4 x 7 7/8 ins

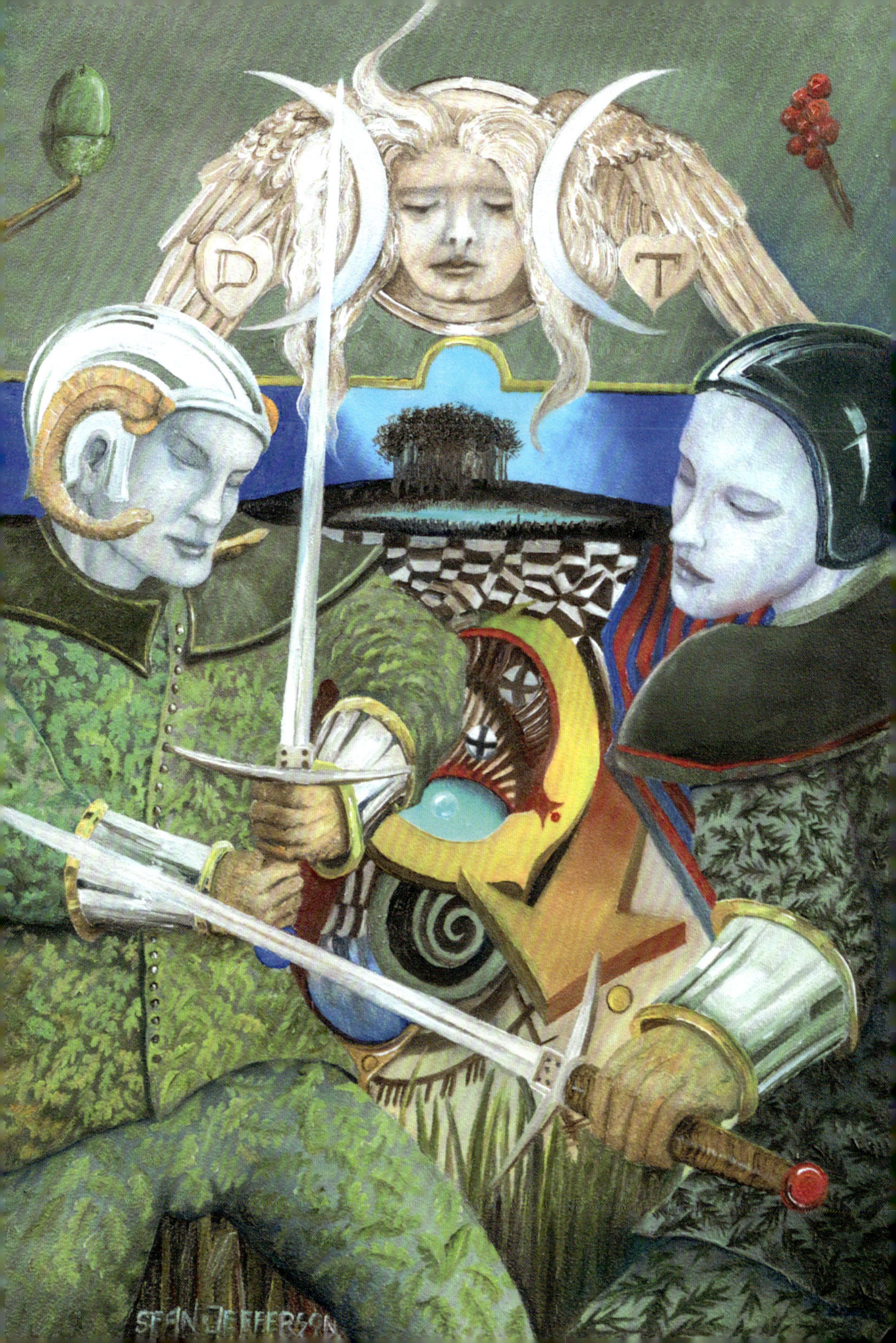
D
T
SEAN JEFFERSON

Three, Three the Rivals

The Symbolism in this painting represents the three belief systems which arose out of the three major phases in the evolution of human society and have survived as rival subcultures, and/or the dominant culture.

Firstly there was Hunter Gatherer society which venerated personified forms of Nature Spirits.

Secondly, Agrarian society where time measured by the Luna months and the phases of the moon dictated crop sewing and harvesting.

Thirdly the rise of City States ruled by powerful rich elites who venerated the sun. The yearly death and rebirth of the sun, and it's journey through the underworld every night, fitting with their beliefs in their own reincarnation into an afterlife.

4

Three. The Rivals

oil on board

30 x 20 cms 11 3/4 x 7 7/8 ins

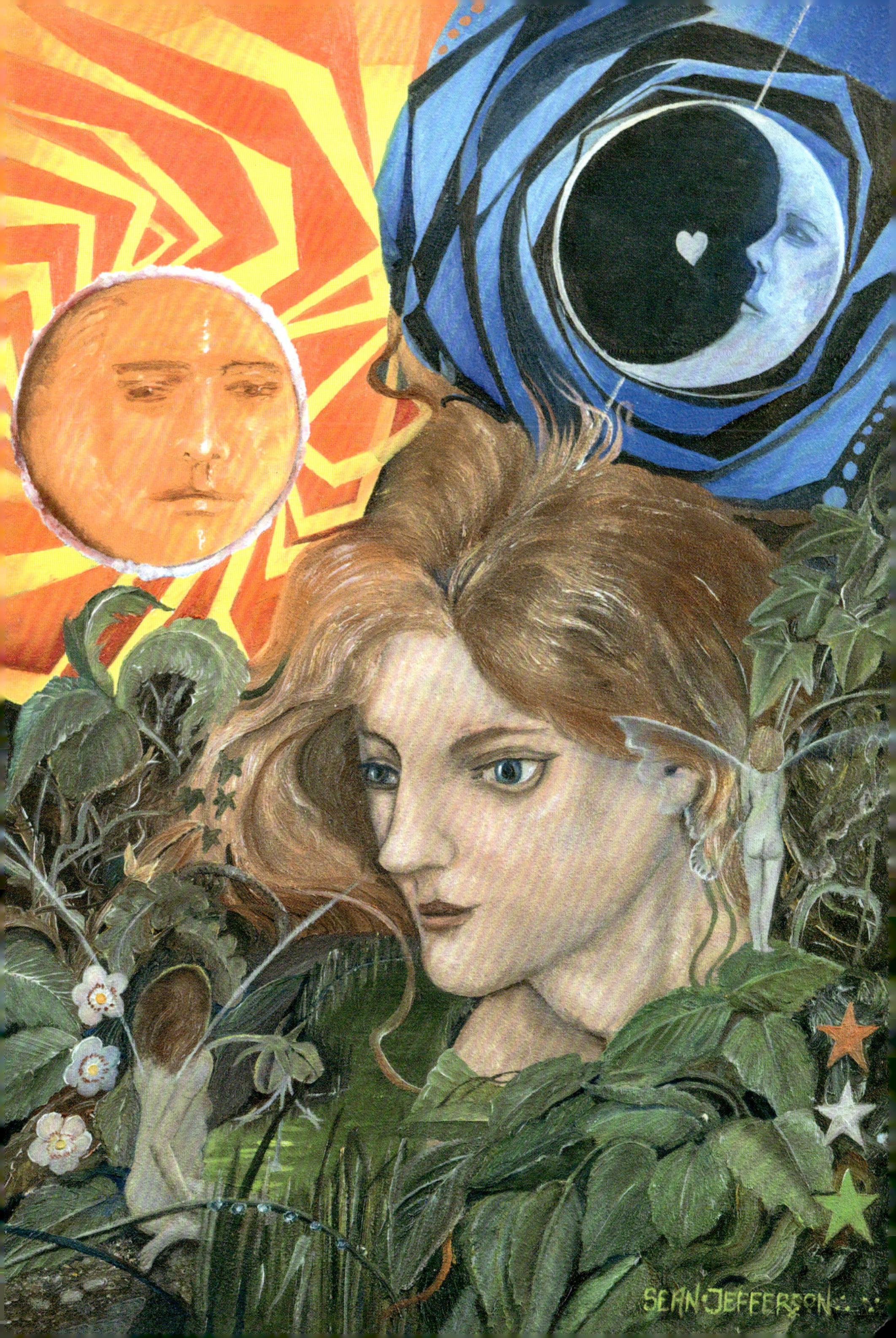
SEAN JEFFERSON

Four for the Gospel Makers

The authorship of the four canonical gospels are traditionally Matthew, Mark, Luke and John.

The four are one of the main symbols in Christian iconography, represented not as men but four winged creatures in what is known as a tetramorph. In the context of the song, I felt this would make the best image. It seems to have an almost talismanic property. The winged creatures are often described as Cherubim, a class of winged angels.

Matthew is represented as a winged man. Mark a winged lion. Luke a winged Ox or Bull. John an Eagle. These symbolic representations derive from the vision of the Old Testament prophet Ezekiel which was thought by Christians to prefigure the coming of Christ.

The old prayer 'Matthew, Mark, Luke and John, bless the bed that I lie on' goes on to ask for the presence of four Angels and like the tetramorph has the feel of a magic charm.

The St Brigid's Cross, Cros Bríde in Irish, is woven out of rushes on St Brigid's Day, February 1st, and is a protective charm. St Brigid was later removed as a Saint as she had been a Bishop in the earlier Celtic Christian Church. Her earliest incarnation was as one of the most powerful of the Pagan Irish Goddesses.

5

Four. Gospel Makers

oil on board

30 x 20 cms $11\frac{3}{4} \times 7\frac{7}{8}$ ins

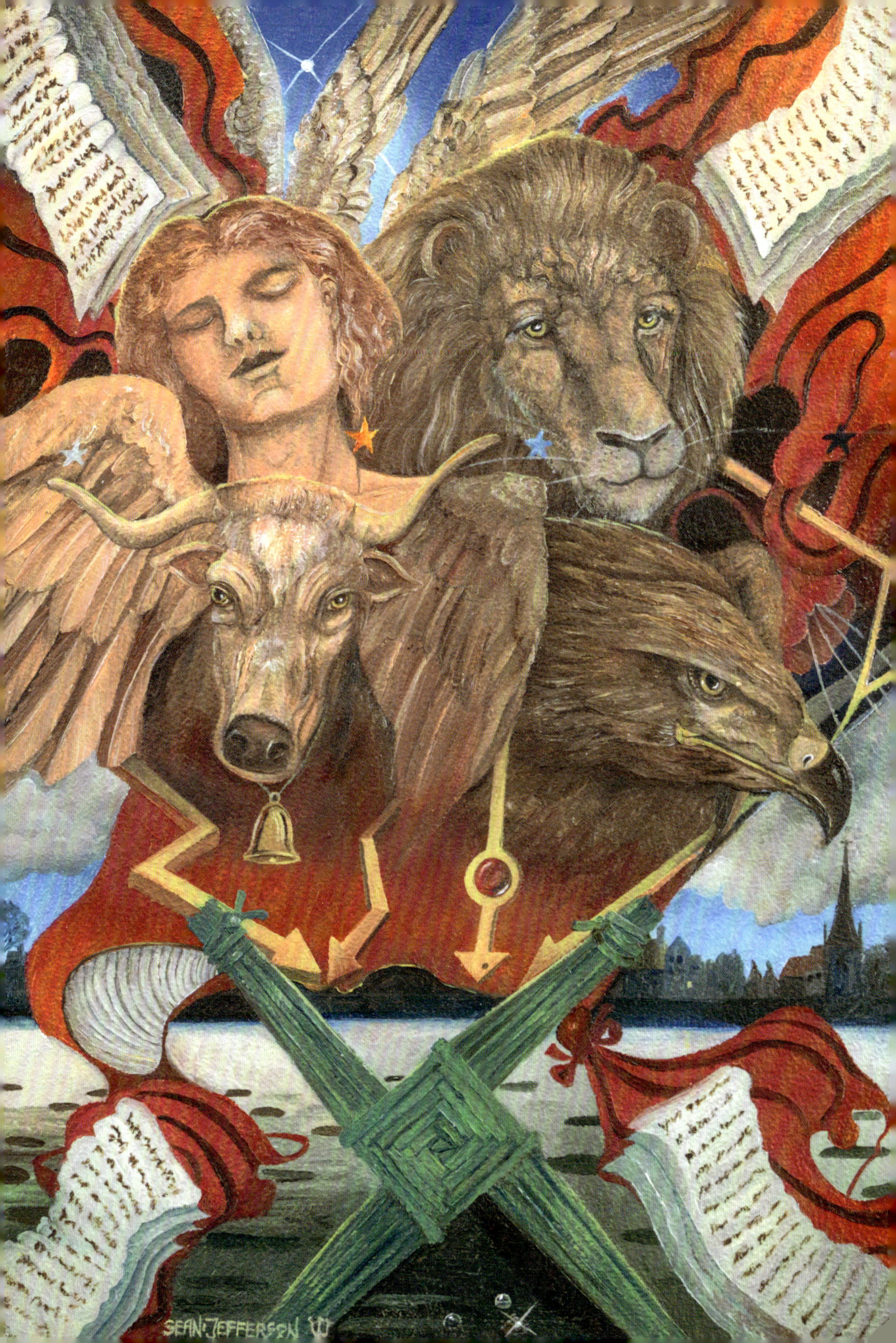
SEAN JEFFERSON

Five for the Symbols at Your Door

To prevent supernatural evil entering a building magical symbols are placed around the door or sometimes fireplace.

In this instance the evil is represented by a young Witch, her Fairie green dress alive with imps and spirits, all under her control, accompanied by her blue cat familiar.

One of the most potent protective symbols in magic is the five pointed star, but be careful to have a single point uppermost. For the symbols on the top step, I allowed the spirit which often works through me to transcribe the first and third, and the last symbol is the Elizabethan Magus, John Dee's Hieroglyphic Monad, which encompasses each symbol of the classical planets.

The symbols along the rise of the step are some of the mysterious symbols to be found on kerb stones, largely in and around Lincoln's Inn Fields and Clerkenwell in London.

6

Five. Symbols at Your Door

oil on board

30 x 20 cms $11\frac{3}{4} \times 7\frac{7}{8}$ ins

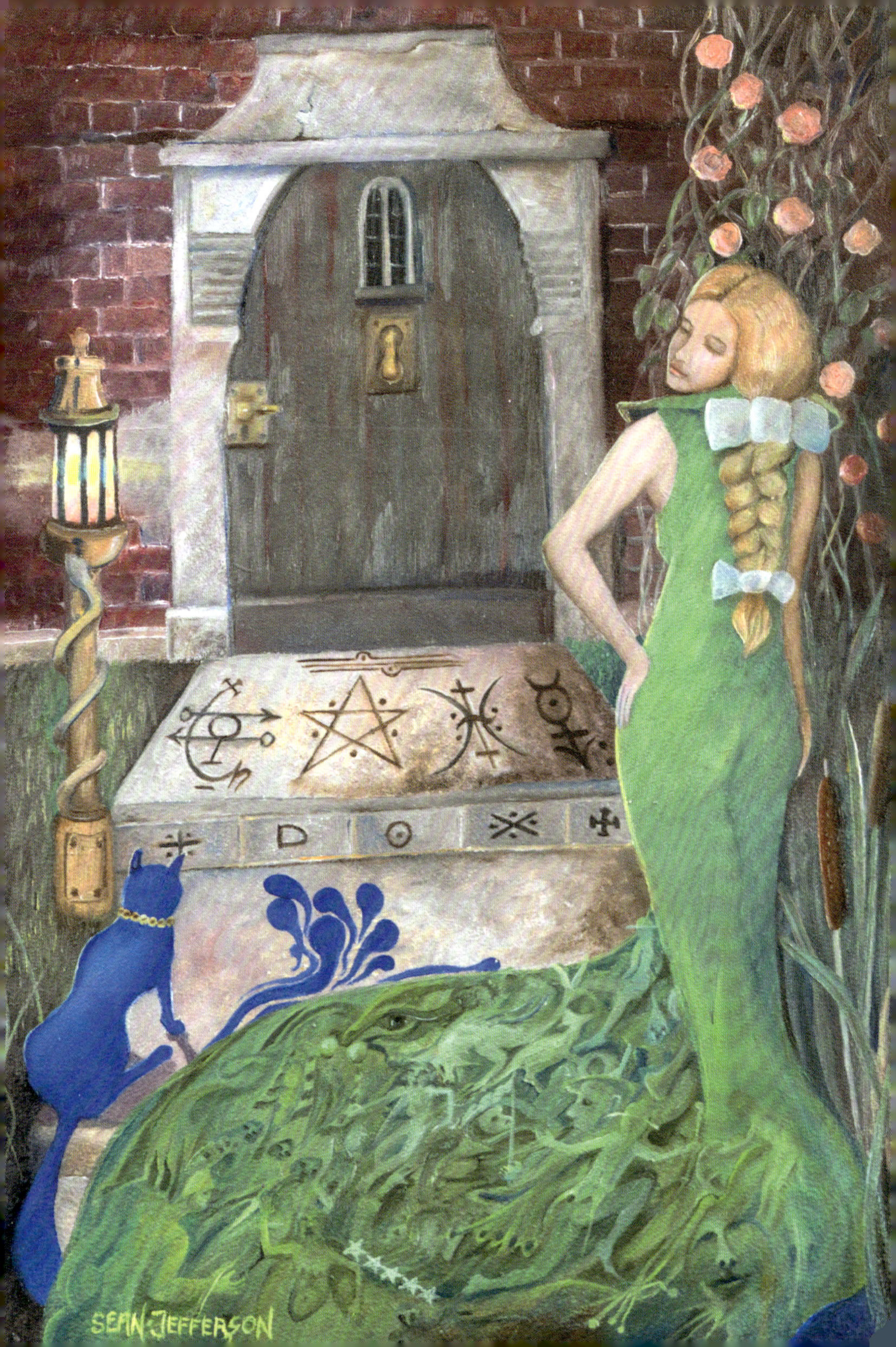
SEAN JEFFERSON

Six for the Six Proud Walkers

I have deviated from the more common interpretation of this verse, as this represents the Burghers of Calais, the six city leaders of Calais who offered themselves up for execution in exchange for the sparing of the other inhabitants, after Edward III captured the city in 1346. Edward famously spared the brave Burghers after the intervention of his wife, Philippa of Hainault.

Instead I have kept with the Astrological/Astronomical theme and linked it to 'The Path Direct' series of paintings, a subject to which I occasionally return, based on an observation noted by Austin Osman Spare (see first Messum's Catalogue).

The Proud Walkers here are the Wandering Stars. The classical planets of Astrology minus the Sun which is the fixed point around which they wander.

Each is personified as an Archetype.

I am a great advocate of what is best described as Spiritual Walking in the Countryside, City or Edgeland, it is the sensation of being in two worlds at once, that of Consensual Reality and that of Energised Imagination, a mindset essential for the Symbolist Artist.

7

Six. Proud Walkers

oil on board

30 x 20 cms 11¾ x 7⅞ ins

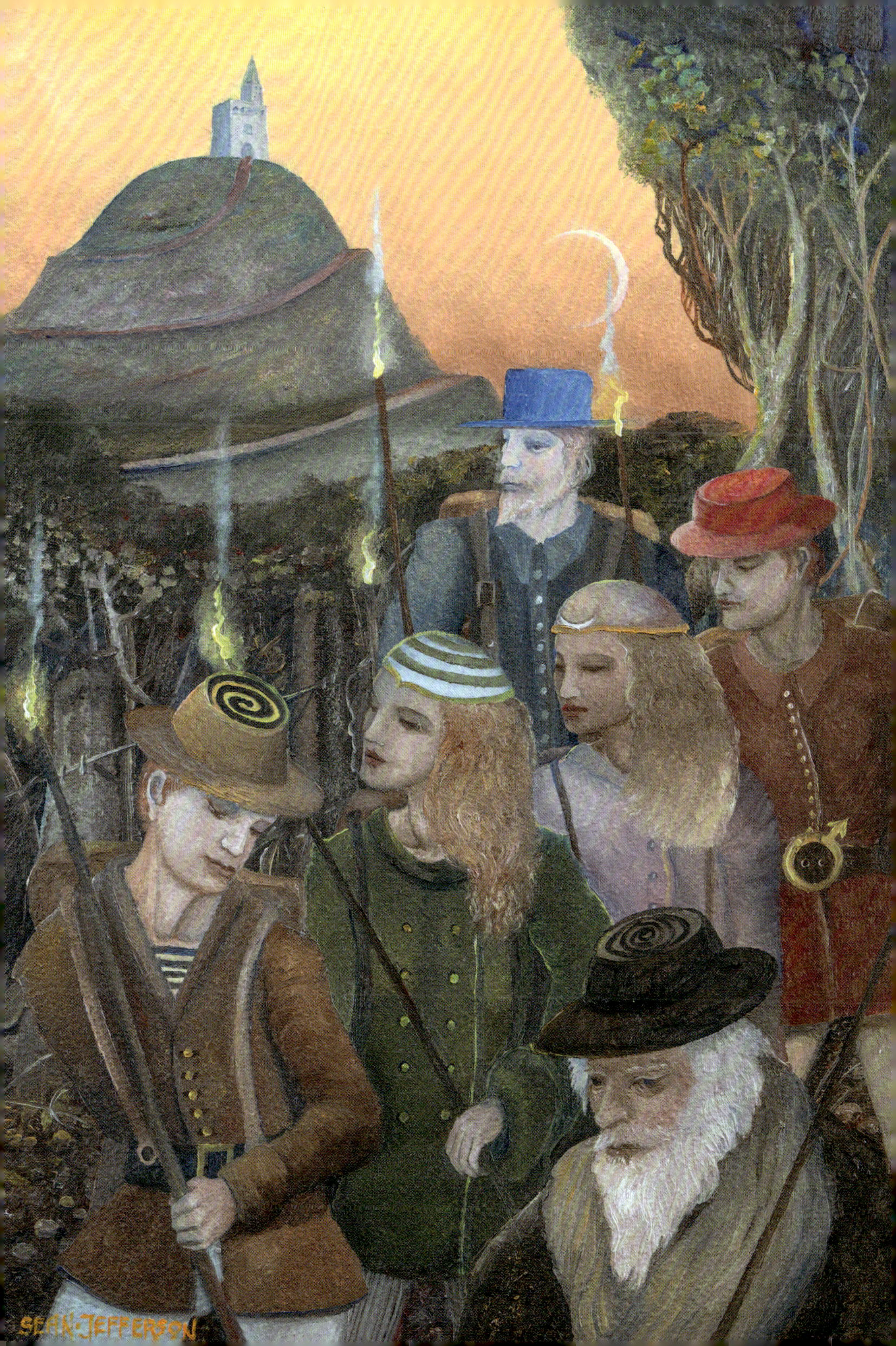
SEAN-JEFFERSON

Seven for the Seven Stars in the Sky

Here we have the Pleiades, or The Seven Sisters the most easily recognised and mysteriously beautiful star constellation. How come only that little patch of sky has so many visible stars?

Each star, in classical mythology, is the personification of a daughter of Atlas. Having to hold up the sky for eternity he was unable to protect his daughters from being raped by the hunter Orion, so Zeus transformed them into the stars we see today except we only now see six with the naked eye.

Astronomers believe that one of the stars Pleione has gradually moved over time and is now so close to the star Atlas that they look like one star. Since the original myth was formulated later generations were taught that one of the daughters fell in love with a mortal and is no longer in position in the night sky.

That Pleione went out of view around 100,000 years ago this would make the Orion story incredibly early, but this is corroborated by similar myths of Orion chasing seven and then only six girls across the sky in cultures from all over the world, most significantly in Native Australian culture where there has been no contact with other cultures with the same myth until very recent times.

In my painting my Indian Pi Dog features as one of the earliest Dog breeds, first bred around 300BC. The Pleiades still taunt Orion dancing above the Oast Houses in the midnight Kent sky.

8

Seven. Stars in the Sky

oil on board

30 x 20 cms   11 3/4 x 7 7/8 ins

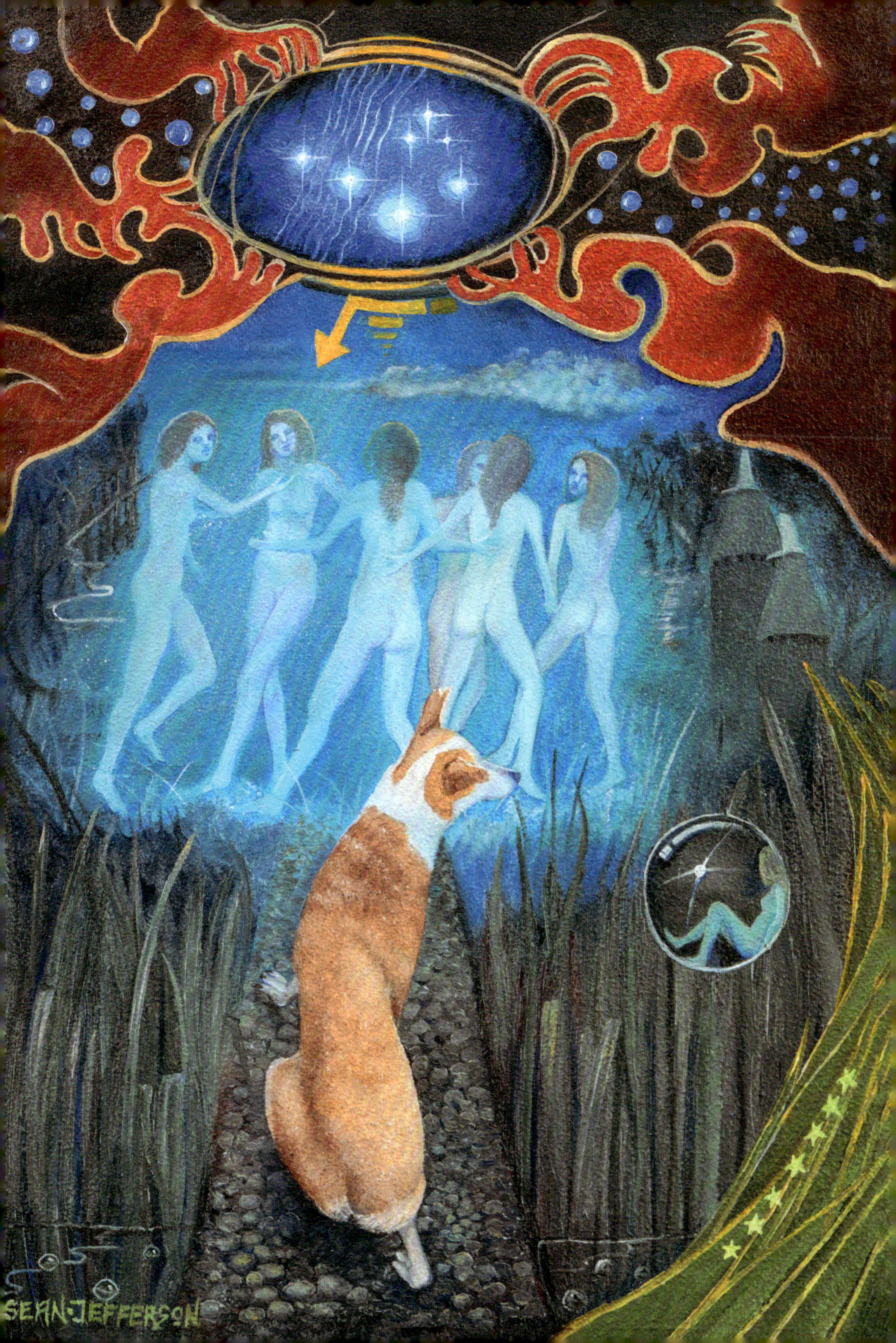
SEAN-JEFFERSON

Eight for the April Rainers

This seems like another straight forward Astrological reference. These are the Rainy Hyades, in classical literature, the V shaped star cluster in the constellation of Taurus.

In April the sun rises in the Hyades and this is the season of April showers vital for the growth of crops.

In keeping with the previous image I have personified the stars as young women. In this image they are generating the rain breaking the flat surface of a lake into the characteristic, strangely hypnotic, moving pattern of intersecting circles.

Whilst working on this image the phrase, ‘ Good weather for ducks’, kept coming into my head.

9

Eight. April Rainers

oil on board

30 x 20 cms   11 ¾ x 7⅞ ins

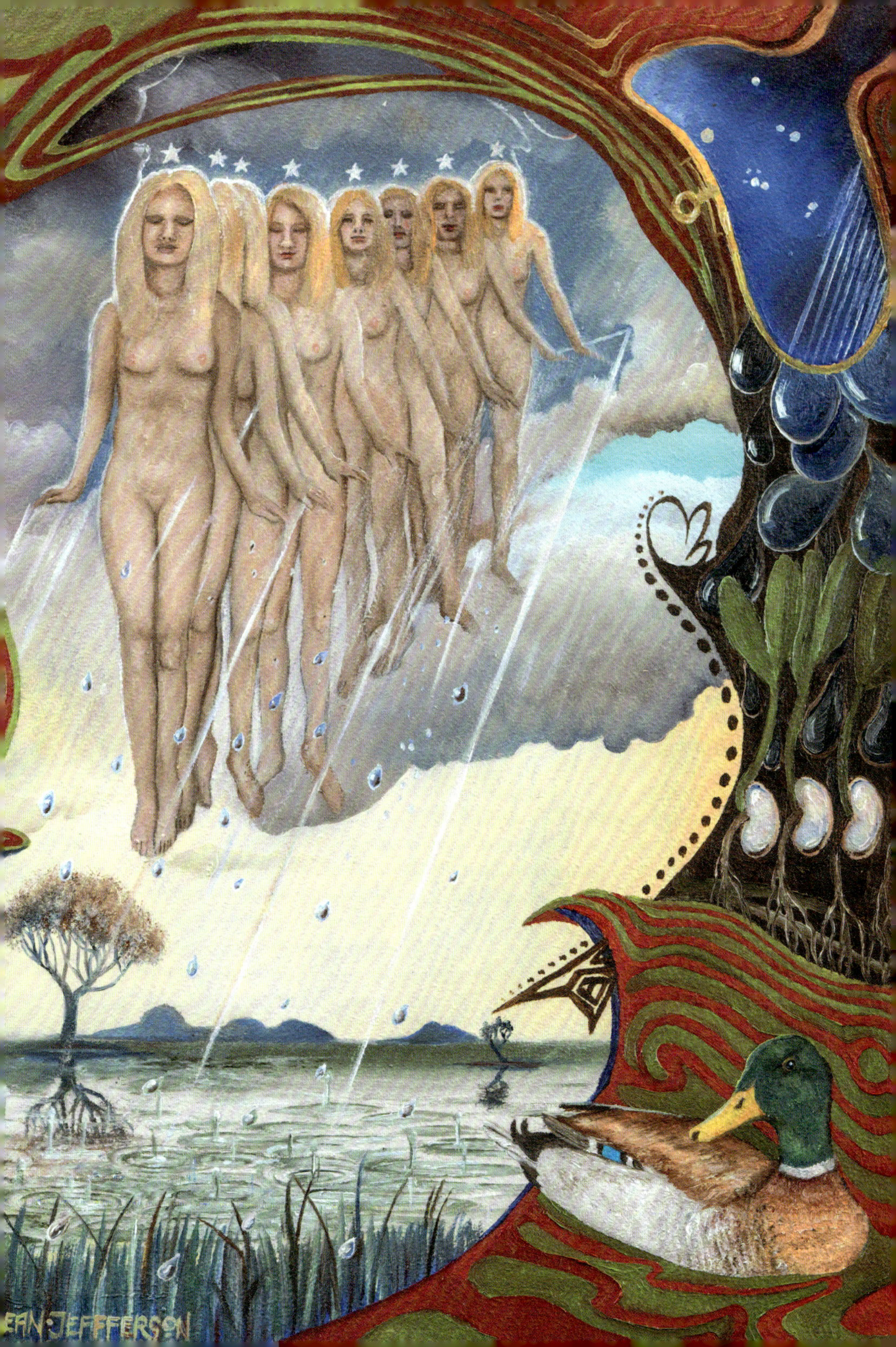
EAN·JEFFERSON

Nine for the Nine Bright Shiners

This verse is usually associated with the Angels.

This is a highly complex subject but I have kept it simple by simply referencing the Angels in 'The Scale of the Number Nine' as given in Francis Barrett's book 'The Magus or Celestial Intelligencer'

William Blake was far from an eccentric artist prone to visionary episodes, often of Angels, he was in fact part of a large group of practicing occultists which included the famous miniaturist Richard Cosway, John Flaxman and the above mentioned Francis Barrett.

I am inclined to think that if there is super intelligent life somewhere in the Universe or unseen dimensions of a Multiverse and that there has been contact with humanity, then the account referring to The Watchers (Angels) in the Book of Enoch is an account of such contact.

The Book of Enoch nearly made it into the Bible and is a fascinating read, especially, as with the Pleiades story it has many echoes in disparate societies.

In my image the Shiners are just that, mysterious lights in the sky, possibly the Angels named in the top left of the painting.

(Note. In my youth I tried to contact Angelic beings using the Enochian language received by John Dee and his Scryer Edward Kelly, a shewstone and, so called, watchtowers in accordance with the recently published Golden Dawn knowledge papers. Instead of Angels I received a vision of myriads of diminutive fairies. This was long before I became aware of the work of Richard Dadd and then much later still, discovered in their first experiment Dee and Kelly had a similar vision although they went on to make contact with what they considered to be Angels, notable for their strict social hierarchy mirroring Elizabethan society.)

10

Nine. Bright Shiners

oil on board

30 x 20 cms 11 3/4 x 7 7/8 ins

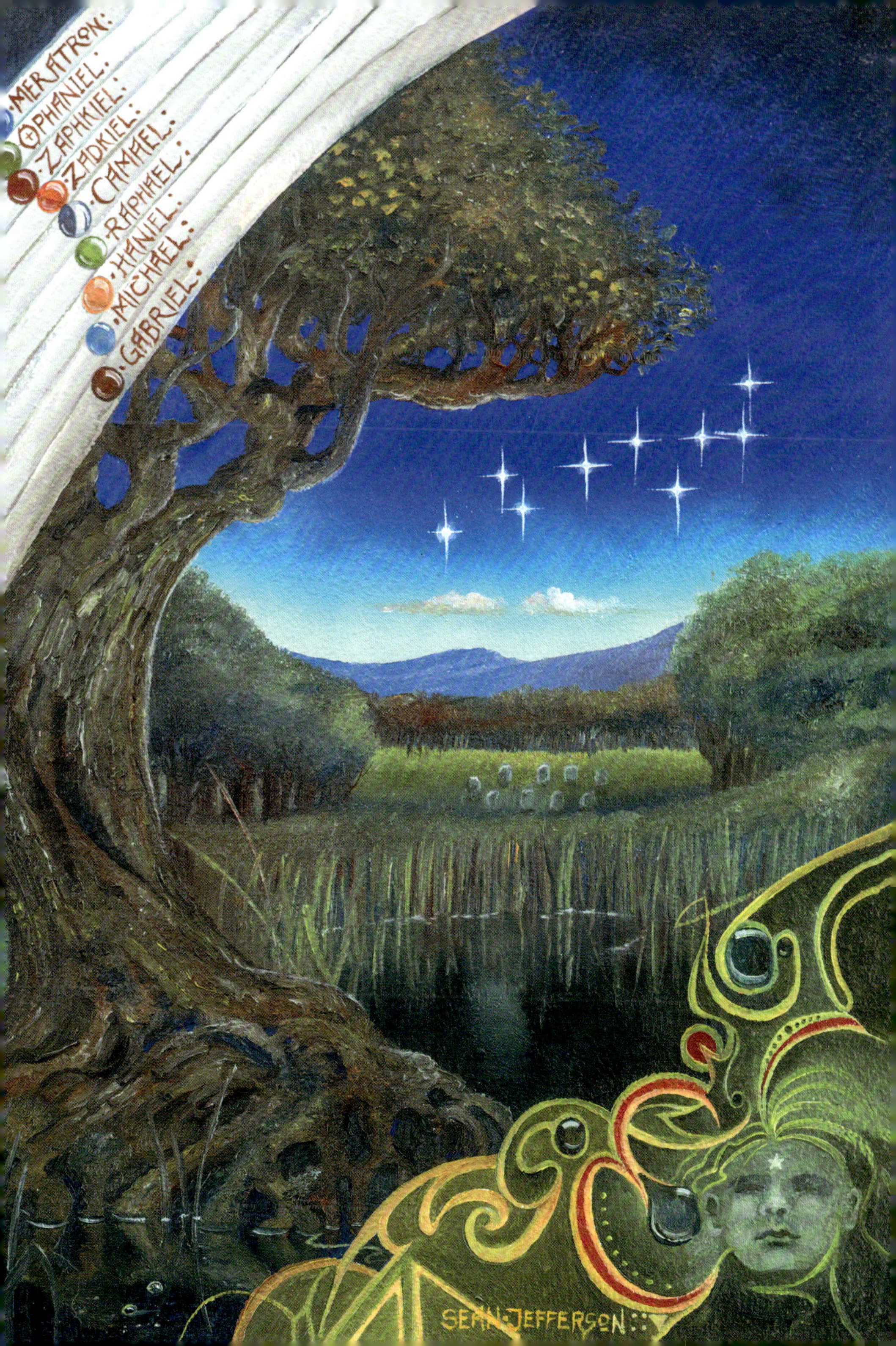
·MERATRON:
OPHANIEL:
·ZAPHKIEL:
·ZADKIEL:
·CAMAEL:
·RAPHAEL:
·HANIEL:
·MICHAEL:
·GABRIEL:
SEAN·JEFFERSON

Ten for the Ten Commandments

Here we are on much firmer ground. The fearsome Patriarch, Moses starting out life in a basket made of rushes and discovered by Pharaoh's daughter in the bullrushes is probably key in the real, now lost, overall meaning of the song. The parting of the Red Sea may well be a mistranslation of parting the Reed Sea.

Moses receives the ten commandments, engraved on two stone tablets by the hand of God. Whilst away receiving the commandments the people of Israel under the influence of Moses' brother take up worshiping The Golden Calf. Enraged by this Moses smashes the tablets and ultimately has those who worshipped the calf killed.

The story goes on but is way beyond my painting. I have kept with the angel theme which seems to run throughout with the inclusion of the Arc of the Covenant. This contains the Tablets of The Law and on top of the Arc is the Mercy Seat from which The Lord spoke to Moses with a Cherubim, winged angel, on each side.

11

Ten. Ten Commandments

oil on board

30 x 20 cms $11\frac{3}{4} \times 7\frac{7}{8}$ ins

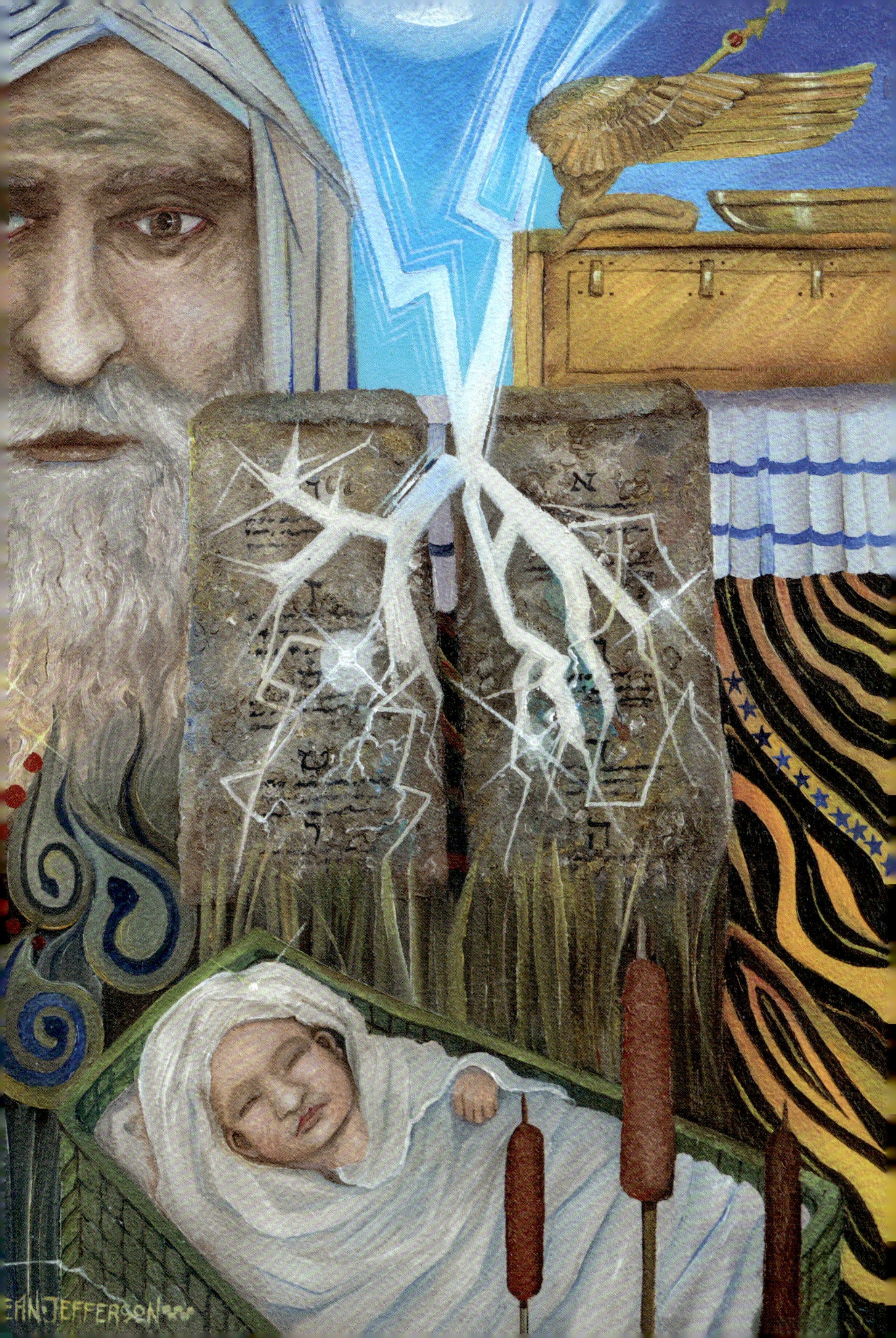
JEFFERSON

The Eleven that Went to Heaven

It is possible that the last two verses are later additions as some versions of the song don't have them. That heaven rhymes with eleven may be the sole reason for its inclusion

It is hard to find much good to say about the number 11 existing as it does between the nicely balanced numbers 10 and 12, described in the Jewish Qabala as 'The unholy 11 is the 11 crowns of impurity'. The ten Sephiroth of the tree of life are added a mysterious eleventh which occupies a central position in the Veil of the Abyss which separates the top three, Supernal Sephiroth, which are in some ways analogous to the Holy Trinity of High Christian teaching from the rest of the tree. To attain oneness with God i.e. Heaven the soul has to cross the Abyss.

In my image The Eleven, transformed into bodies of light ascend towards Heaven. The stars above their heads represent the divine spark in all of us which craves reunion with the Godhead, at least in Gnostic mystical belief.

12

Eleven. That went to Heaven

oil on board

30 x 20 cms 11 3/4 x 7 7/8 ins

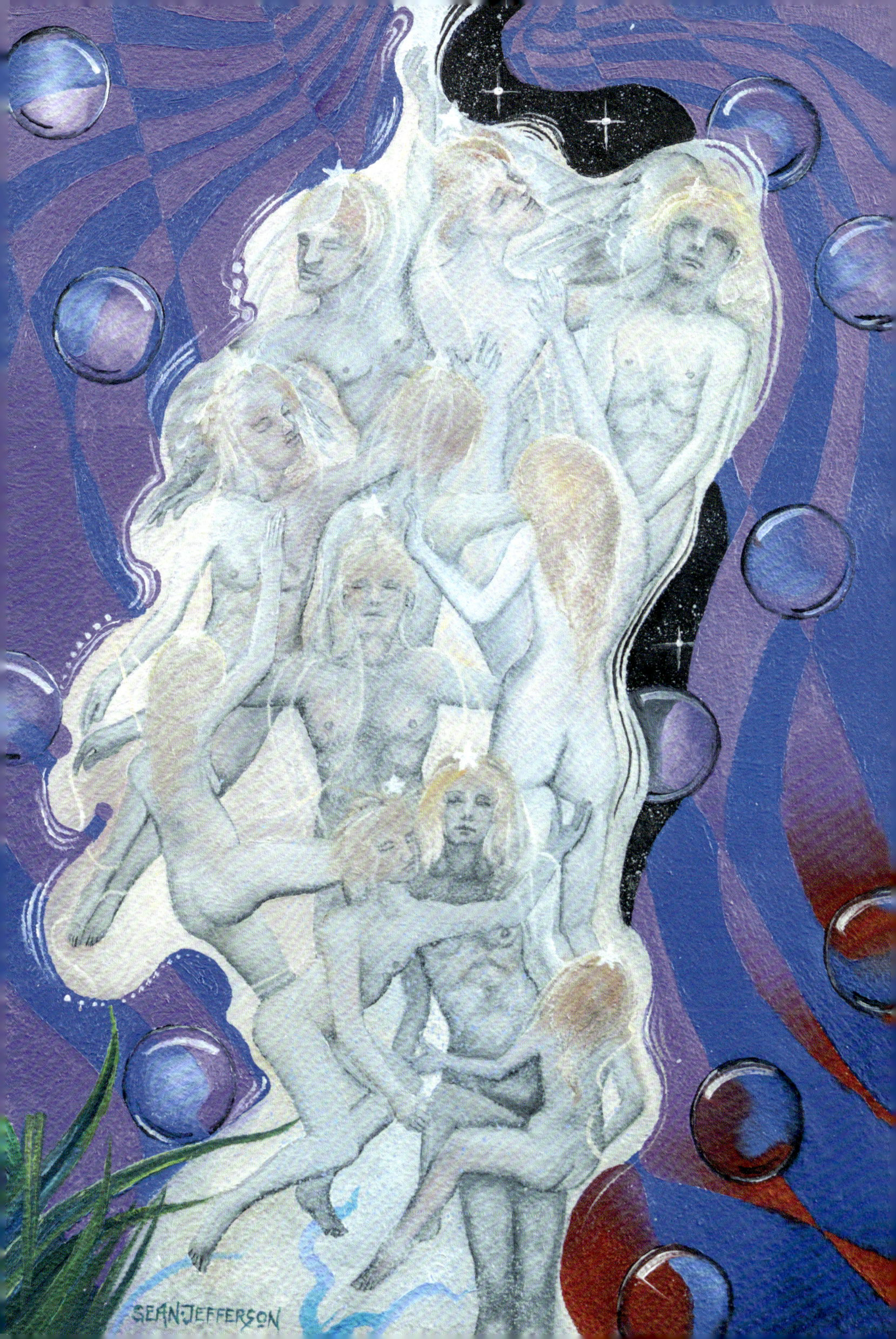
SEANJEFFERSON

Twelve for The Twelve Apostles

This verse is obviously a straight biblical reference, the twelve apostles with Judas replaced by Matthias.

In creating this image I was powerfully moved to place the Apostles around the Mystic Rose, symbol of the Virgin Mary and also central to Rosicrucian symbolism. In keeping with the botanical, rushes thread I have included the various herbs sacred to each Apostle as given by Francis Barrett.

13

Twelve. Twelve Apostles

oil on board

30 x 20 cms $11\frac{3}{4} \times 7\frac{7}{8}$ ins

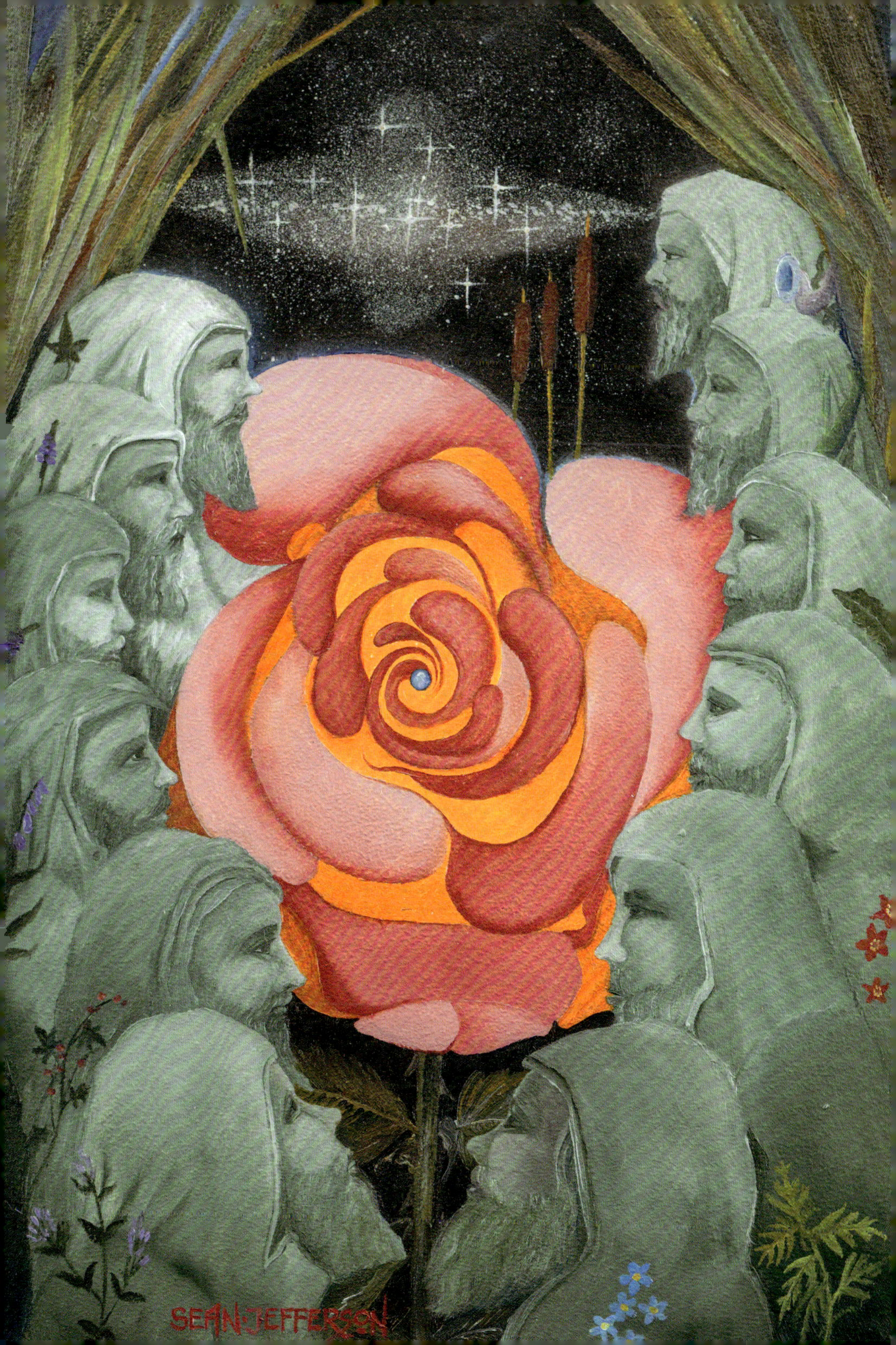
SEAN·JEFFERSON

Commentary on the Magpie Rhyme in its Sevenfold Form and the Related Paintings.

In the British landscape of subtle greens and browns, the sudden appearance of a magpie with its stark black and white plumage is spectacular, and slightly unnerving.

The unnerving psychological response to seeing magpies has led them to be associated with 'Nature Mysteries' and probably led to the composition of the divinatory rhyme (one for sorrow, two for joy, three for a girl, four for a boy, five for silver, six for gold, seven for a secret never to be told). This may also be a survival of Bird Augury, more generalised reading of the intentions of the Fates by the observation of birds and their behaviour, popular with the Romans.

In this cycle of seven paintings I have taken the apparently simple seed concepts of each verse as the starting point of work which draws on Symbolism, Surrealistic improvisation combined with Ruralism and a new take on Psychedelia.

One For Sorrow

One Magpie and a teardrop composition. The sight of one Magpie is thought to bring bad luck and various charms are used to counter the malevolence.

A salute, a wink, or 'Good Morning Mr. Magpie how's your wife' are all said to work, although the latter may only work by confusing heterosexual female and unmarried male birds.

The theme of this work is 'Parting is sweet sorrow', a single lonely bird and a tiny departing ship on the green ocean, reflected in resonating tears and optical invocations of contradictory emotions.

14

One For Sorrow

oil on board

42 x 30 cms 16½ x 11¾ ins

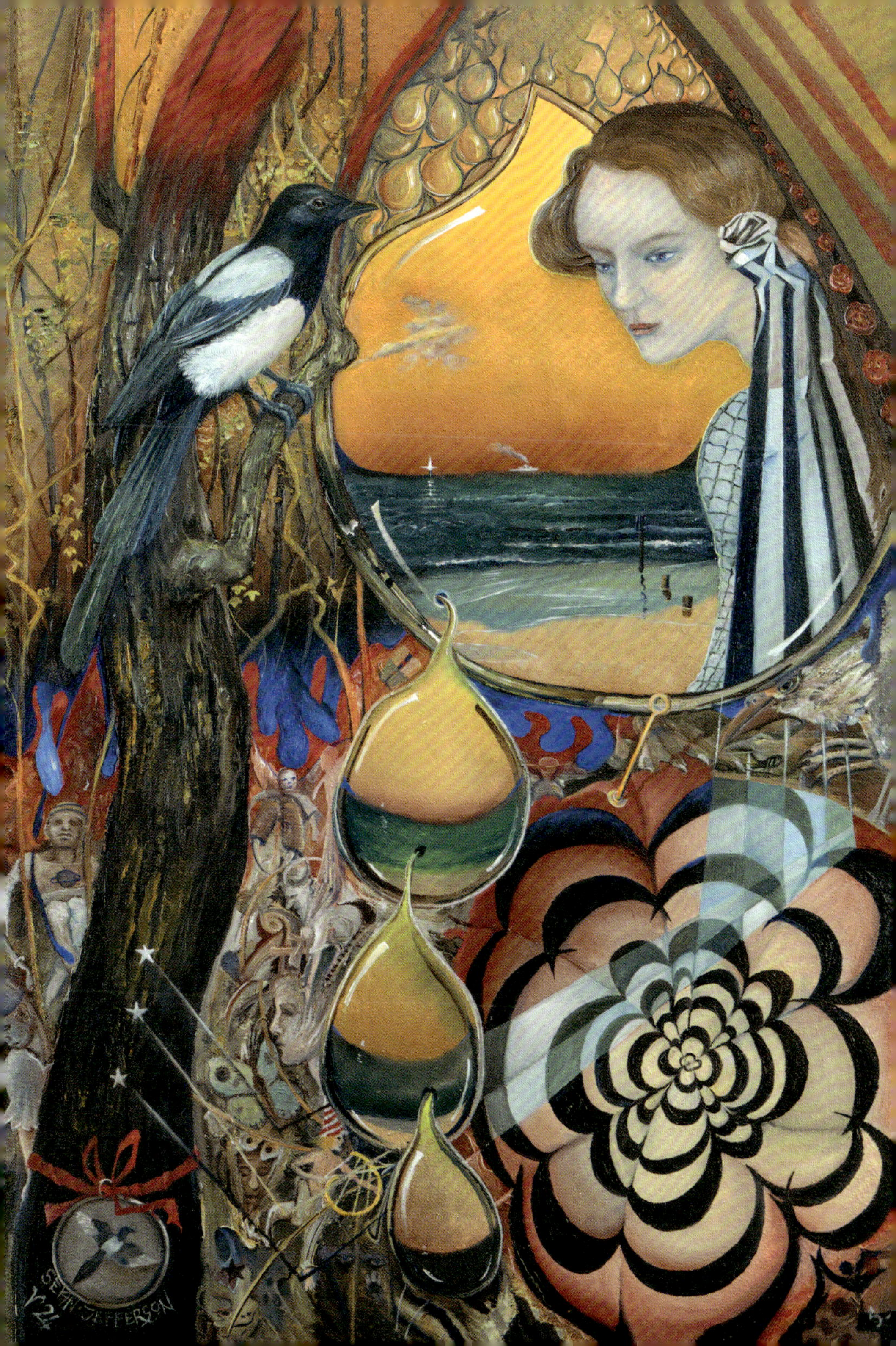
SETH JEFFERSON

Two For Joy

The whole sequence is built around duality, black and white, sorrow and joy etc.

Here we have lovers reunited, symbolising the joy in human relationships, in contrast to the joys of silver and gold, less likely as the number of magpies increases, but actually less valuable. This maybe the 'secret' concealed in appearance of the seven.

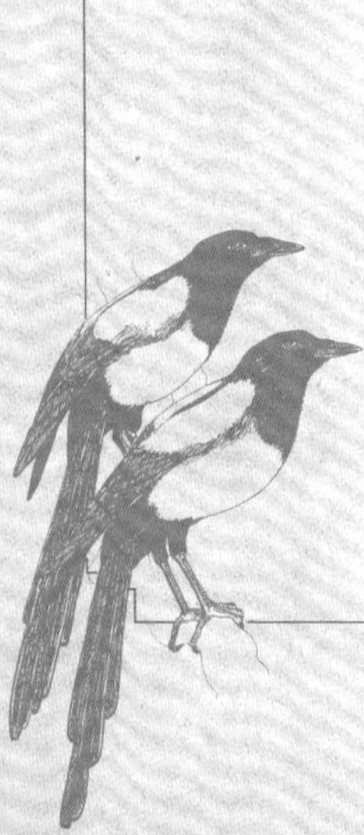

15

Two for Joy

oil on board

42 x 30 cms   16$^{1}/_{2}$ x 11$^{3}/_{4}$ ins

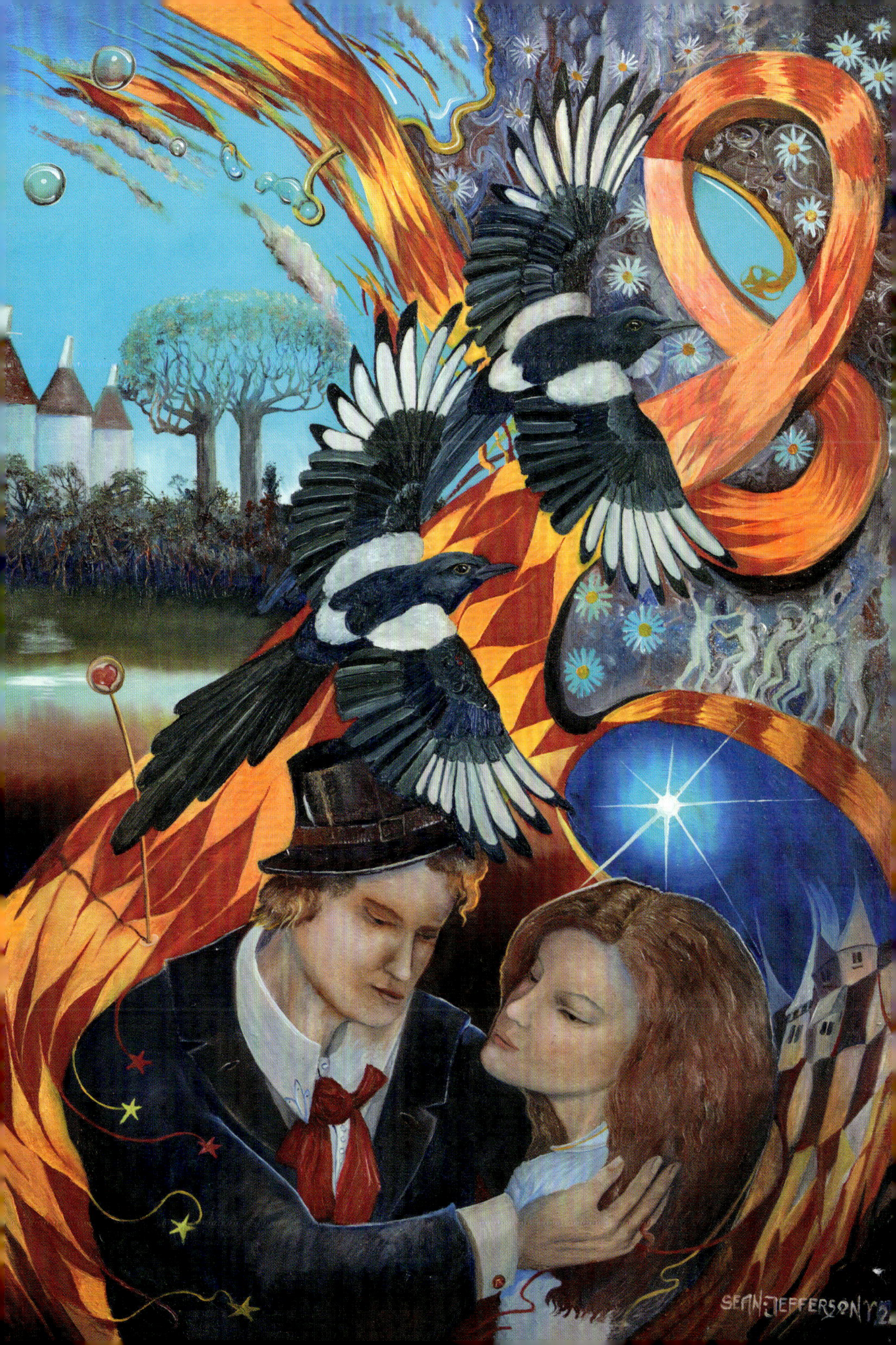
SEAN JEFFERSON

Three For A Girl

In traditional societies the sex of a new born was a vital question and all manner of techniques have been used to determine 'Girl or Boy?'

Possibly the question was asked in some ritualistic manner and then the first Magpie encounter would provide the answer. The whole rhyme may be a folk memory of an ancient system of Natural Magic. A system of belief around a Magpie Totem did exist around the Norse goddess Skadi, Priestess of a Magpie clan.

The painting is based around the most famous girl in the genre of 'serious nonsense', Alice Liddel as photographed by Lewis Carroll.

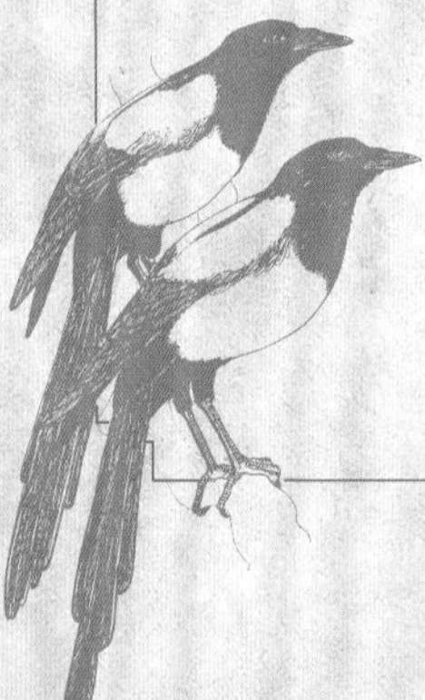

16

Three for a Girl

oil on board

42 x 30 cms 16½ x 11¾ ins

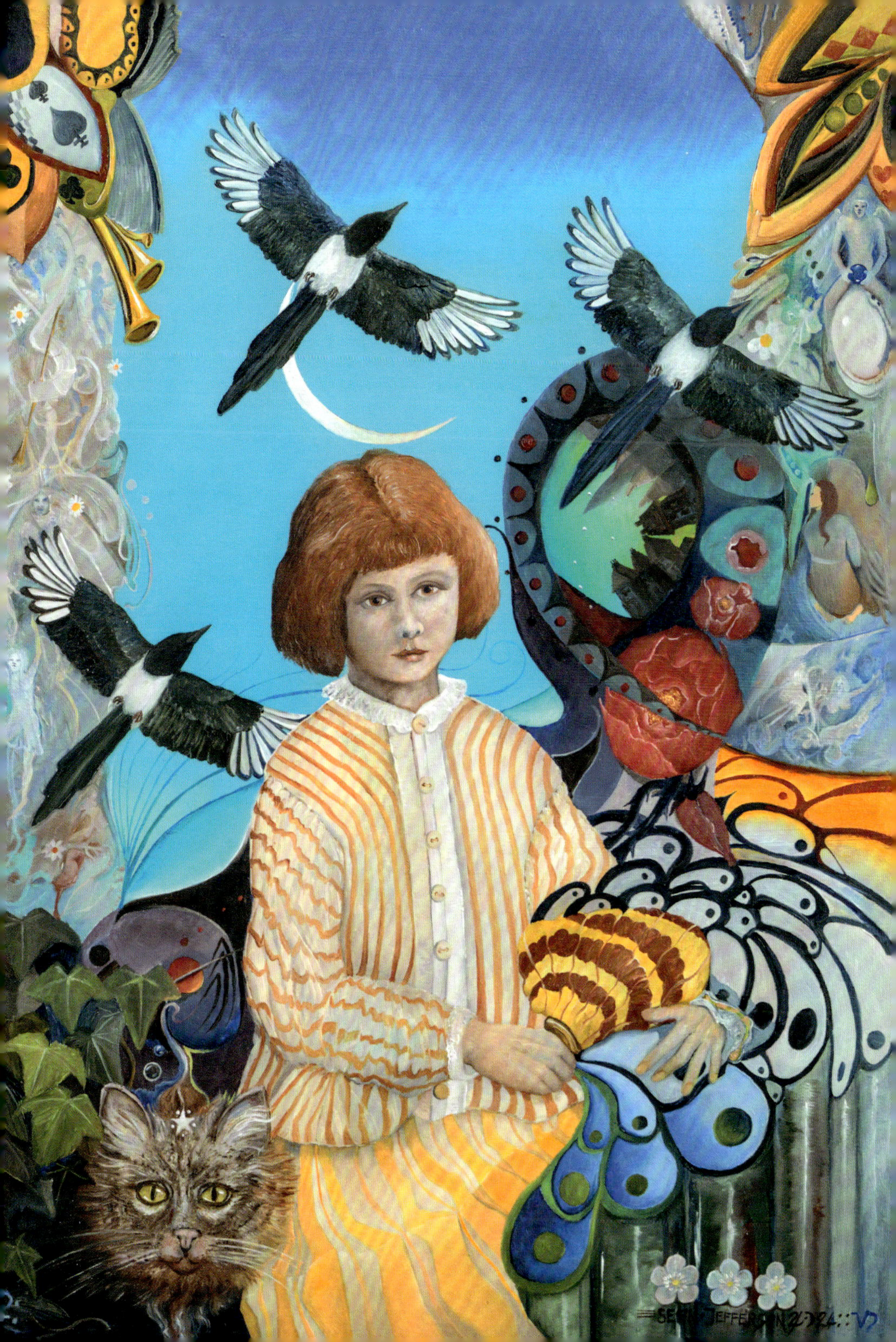

Four For A Boy

Balancing the duality, a group of four magpies being the first seen after asking the 'Girl/Boy' question.

The inspiration for the painting comes additionally from a photograph of Peter Llewelyn Davis, J.M. Barrie's boy who never grew up, Peter Pan, the most famous boy in the genre of 'serious nonsense'.

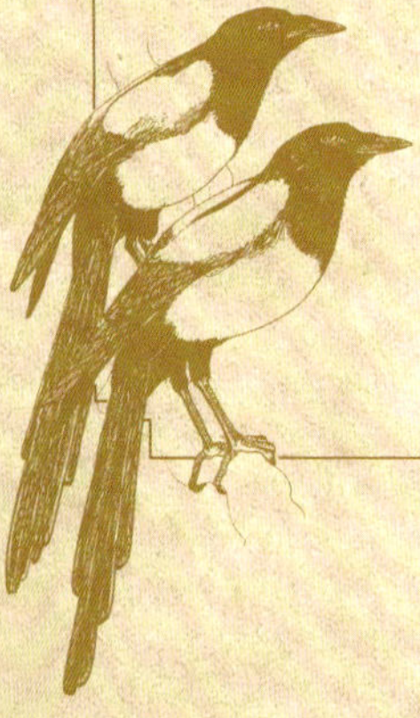

17

Four for a Boy

oil on board

42 x 30 cms   16½ x 11¾ ins

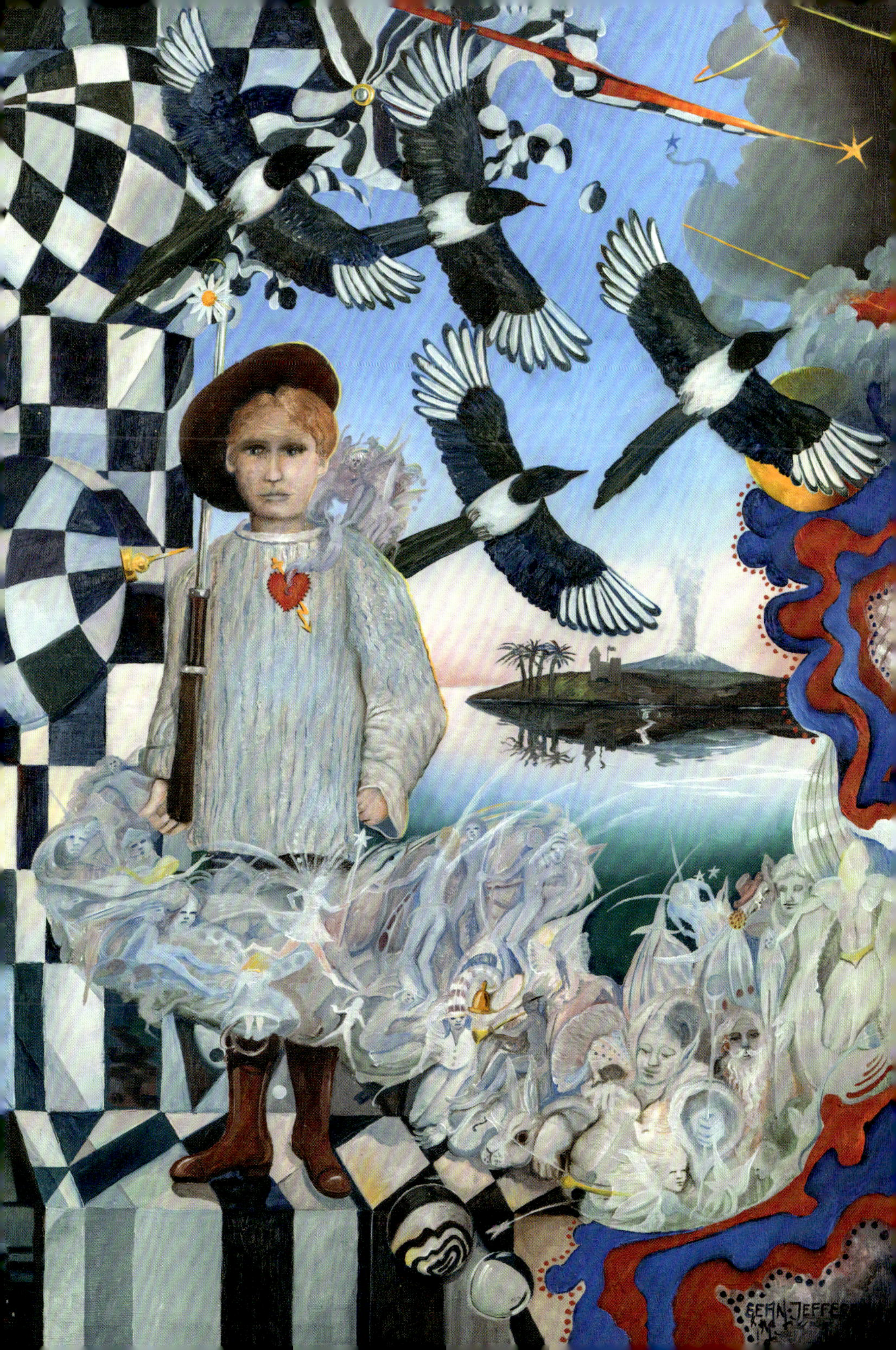

Five For Silver

Half of the Silver/Gold duality, Silver is the metal congruous with the moon, the night and the Female Mysteries.

A talisman featuring five Magpies might be made to attract silver, either literally or in a magical sense.

Five Magpies may predict an increase in wealth but somehow not as much as seeing six and so, as when seeing one for sorrow we find ourselves straining to see an elusive extra bird.

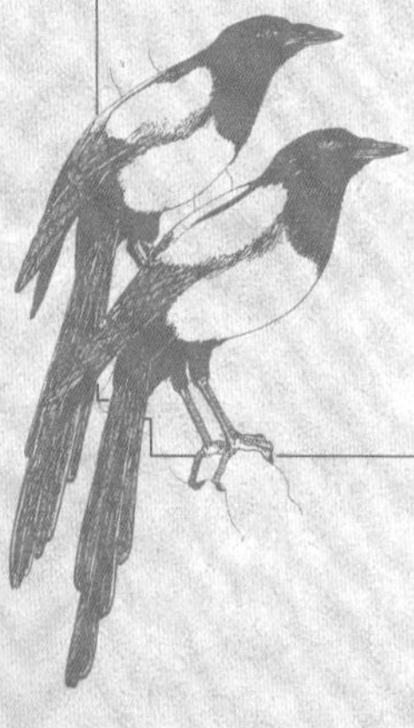

18

Five for Silver

oil on board

42 x 30 cms 16½ x 11¾ ins

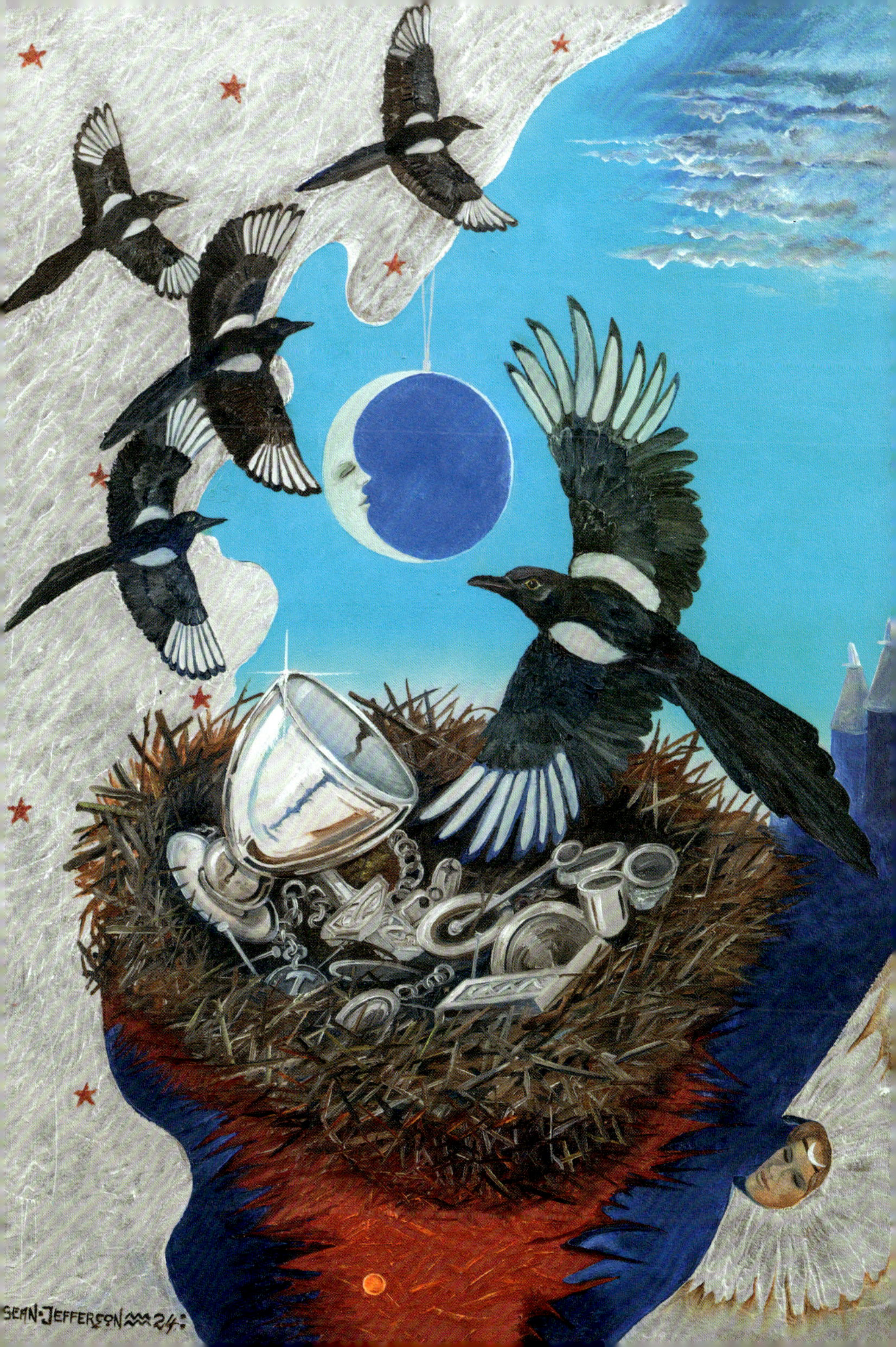
SEAN·JEFFERSON

Six For Gold

It is hard to think of Gold in a magical sense and not think of Alchemy. The similarities between painting and 'The Great Work' are well documented. In its crudest sense taking the seven mundane metals, congruent with the seven classical planets and therefore the seven main psychological archetypes and in the painter's case the seven colours of the visible spectrum and combining them in such a way, and with line, modelling and texture, to produce Philosophical Gold, a Work of Art. The analogue hopefully goes further as the 'Practical Alchemist' attempted to change base metals into gold, so in selling a painting, base materials may be transformed into hard cash.

Encounters with six Magpies prefigure a significant increase in wealth.

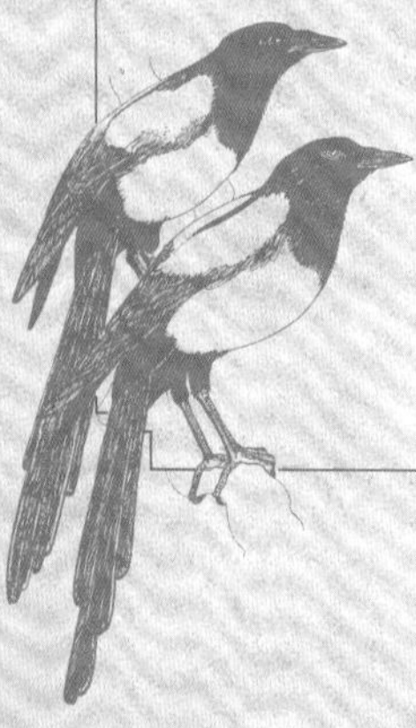

19

Six for Gold

oil on board

42 x 30 cms 16½ x 11¾ ins

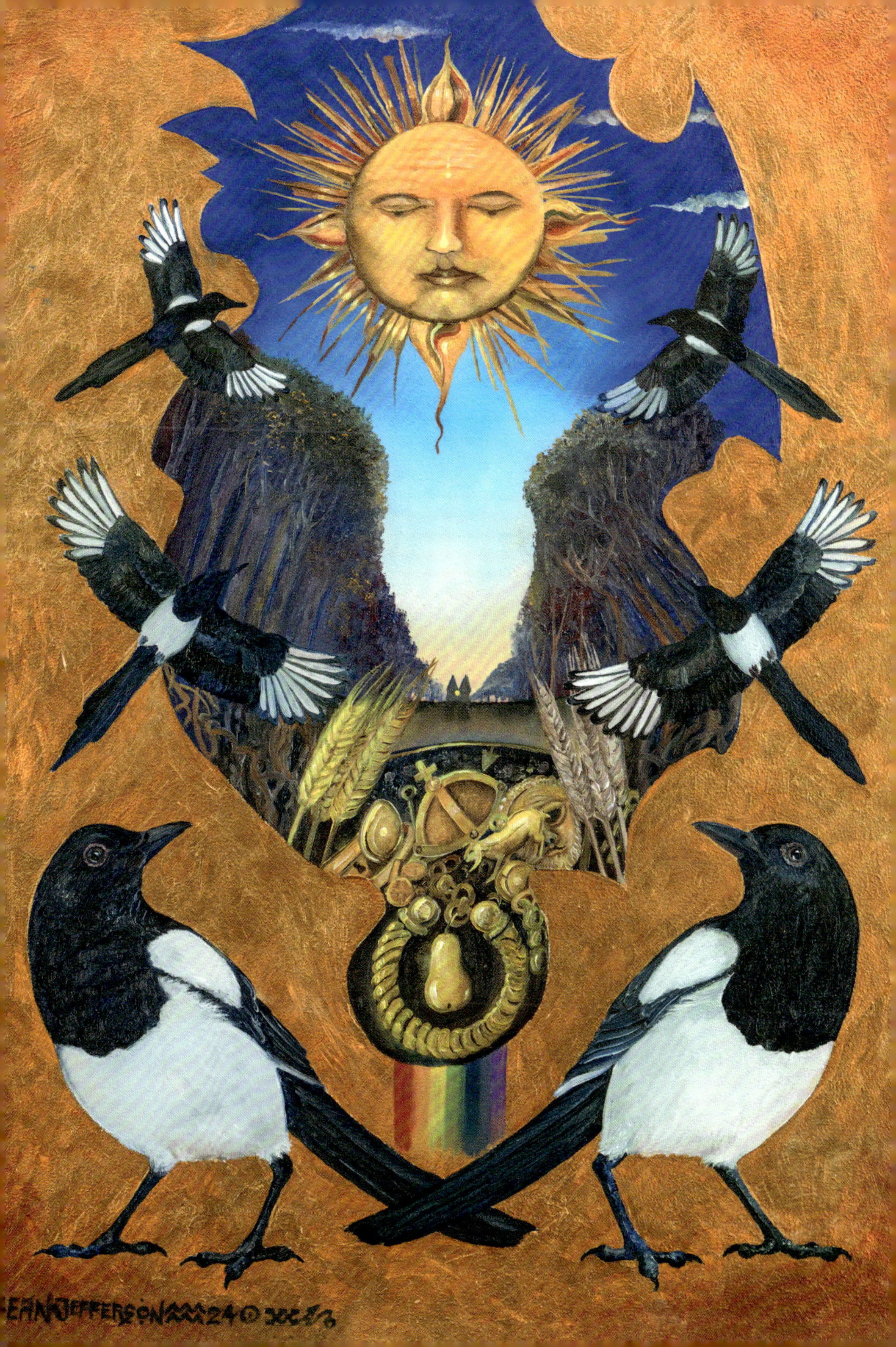
JEFFERSON

Seven For A Secret Never To Be Told

The version of the rhyme I was brought up with ends with seven for a secret.

This implies that the rhyme has greater significance than just a fun way passing time on a long journey.

The number seven corresponds with the seven classical planets and they fit nicely with the symbolism.

Taking the melancholy Saturn for Sorrow, Jupiter the Joy Bringer, A Girl Venus, A Boy Mars, Silver the Moon, Gold the Sun and Mercury in the Greek form Hermes the keeper of the secretive Hermetic Sciences. Each has deep psychological resonances. The secret cannot be articulated as it can only be experienced when consciousness engages with 'wild nature'.

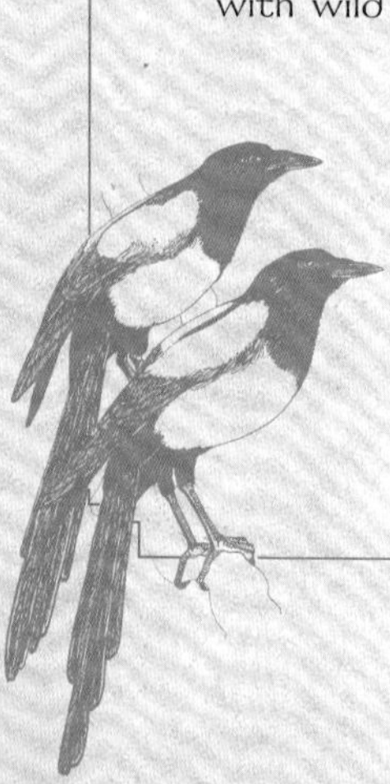

20

Seven for a Secret

oil on board

42 x 30 cms 16½ x 11¾ ins

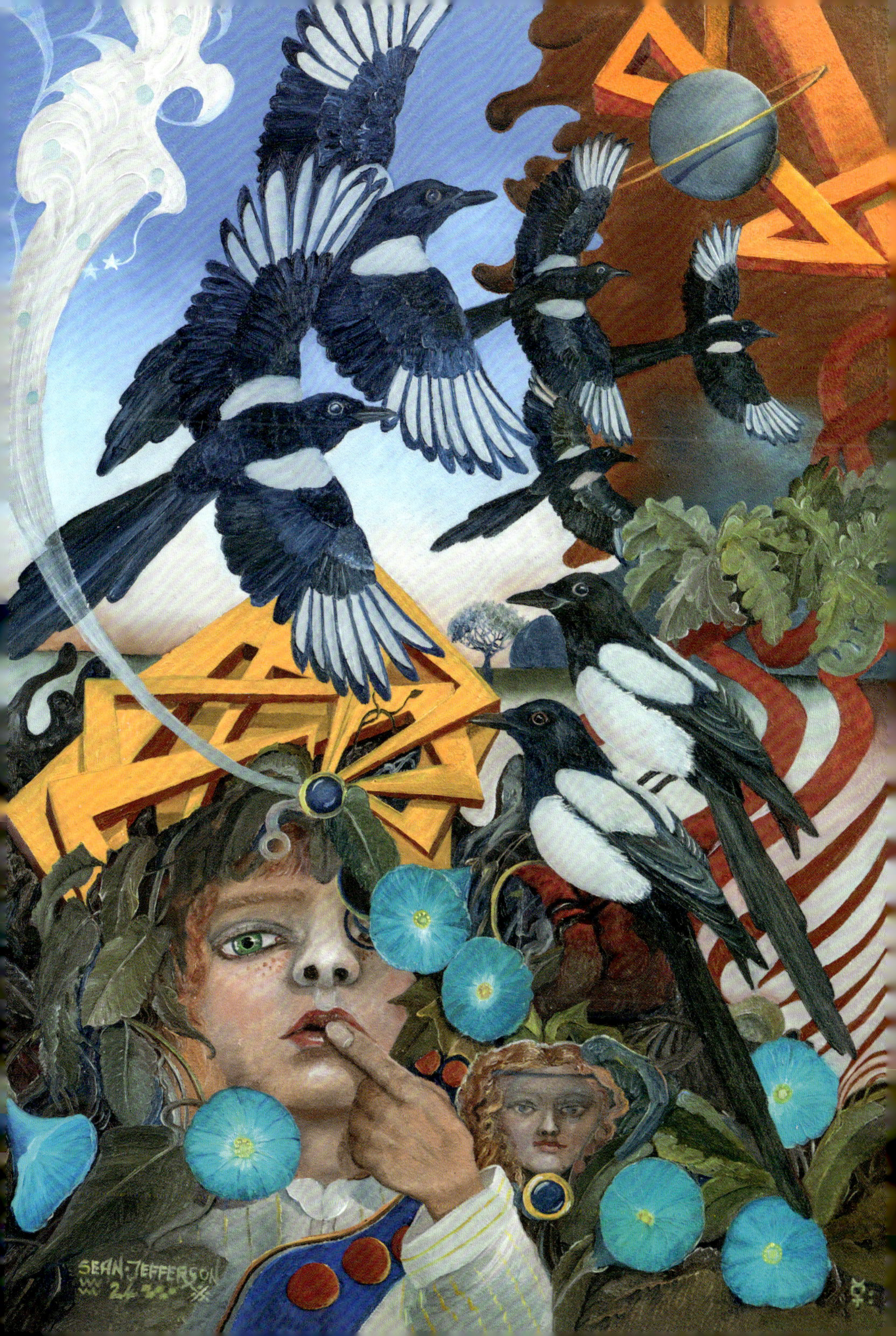
SEAN JEFFERSON
24

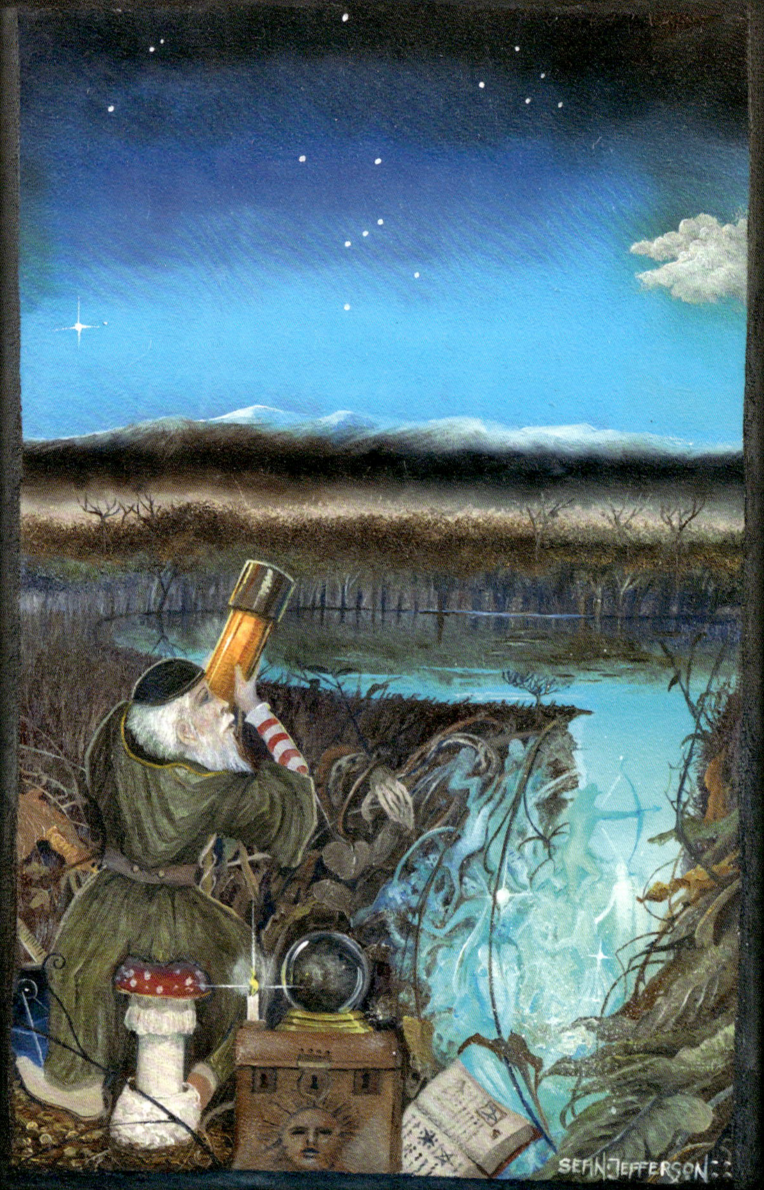

21

A Fairie Astrologer

oil on board

30 x 20 cms $11^{3}/_{4}$ x $7^{7}/_{8}$ ins

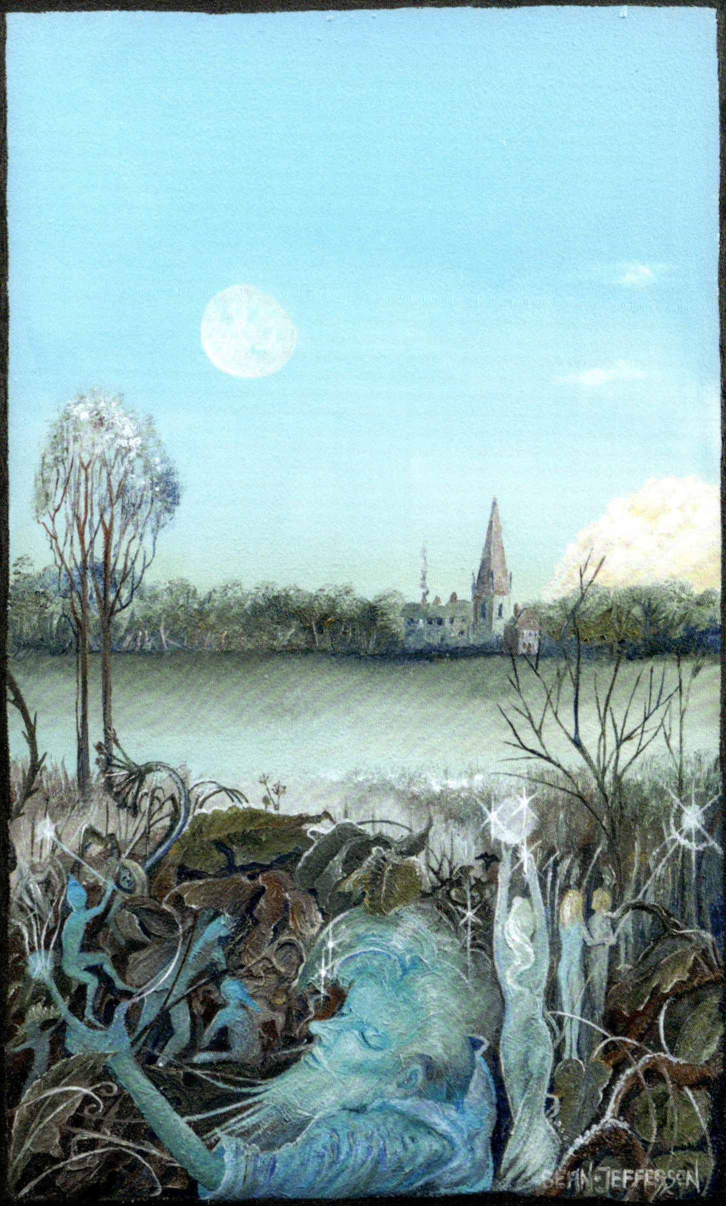

22

Jack Frost Visits Kent

oil on board

30 x 20 cms $11^3/_4$ x $7^7/_8$ ins

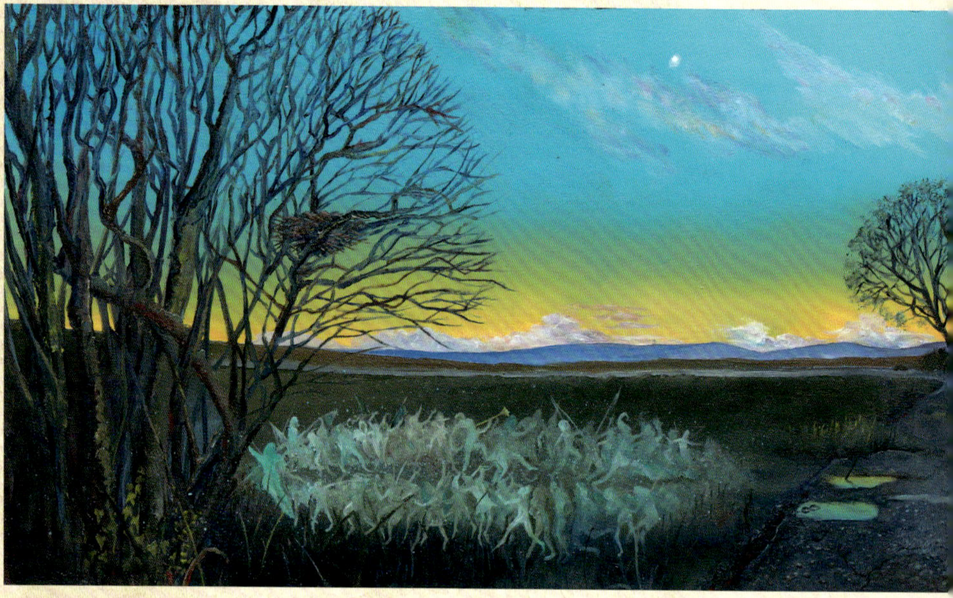

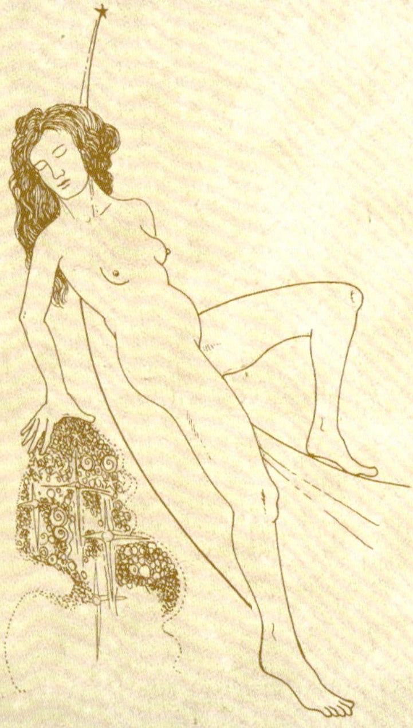

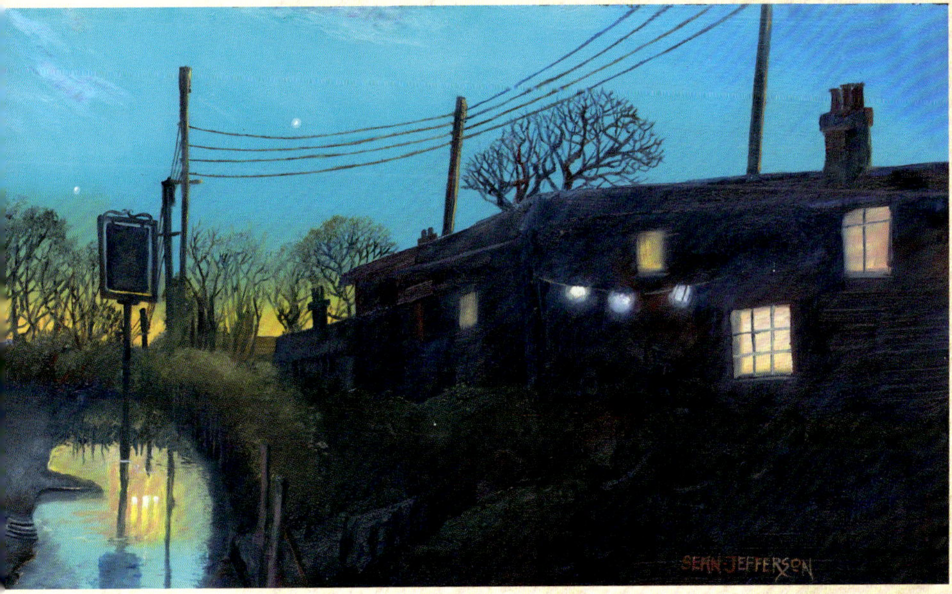

23

Fairy Ring Seen Outside the Ship Inn

oil on board

20 x 69 cms $7^{7}/_{8}$ x $27^{1}/_{8}$ ins

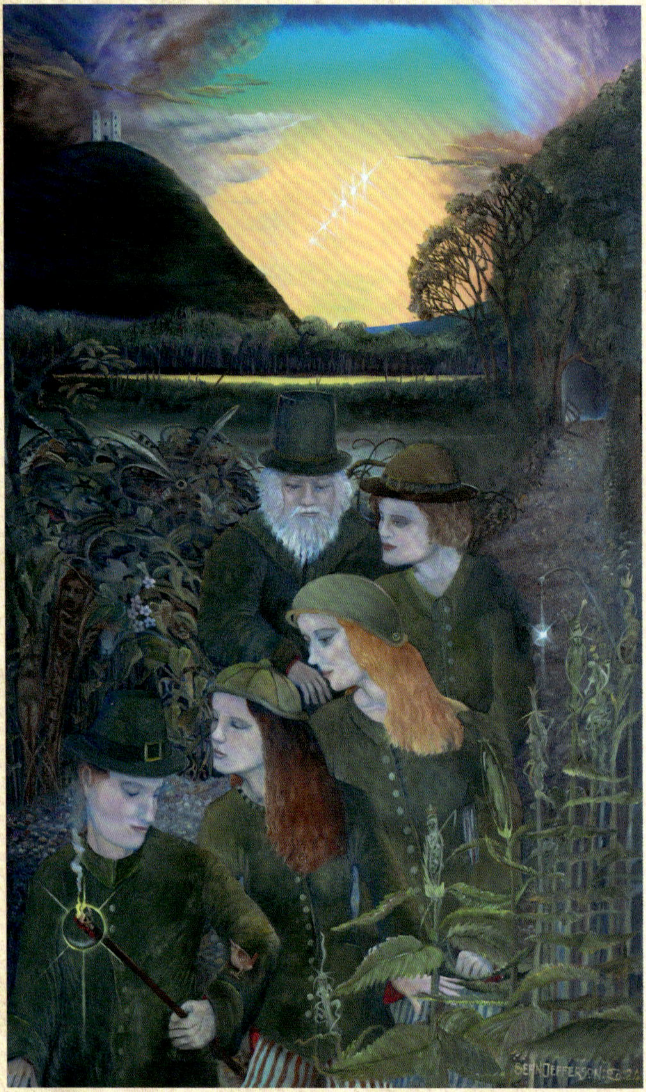

24

For those who Strayed from the Path Direct, no. 3

oil on board

61 x 37 cms   24 x 14⅝ ins

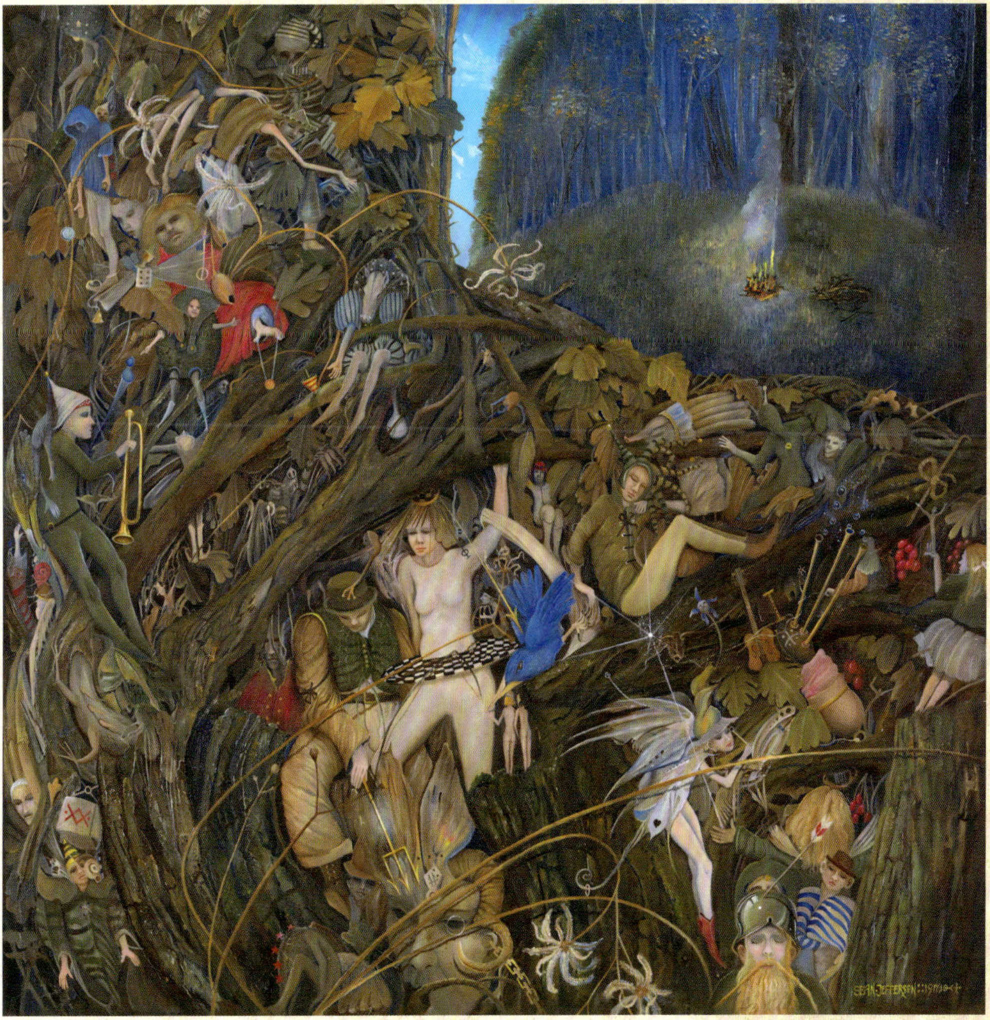

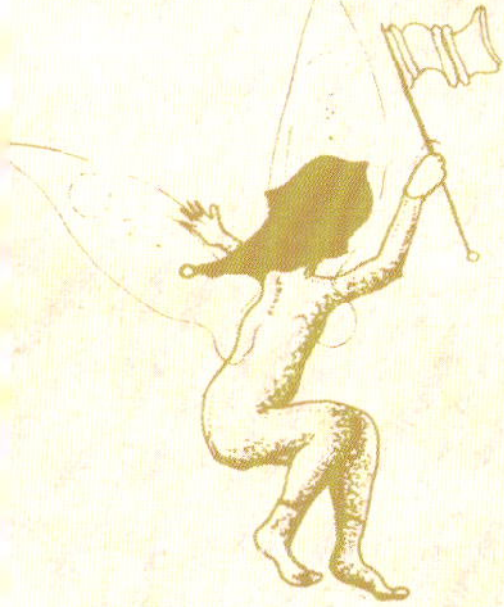

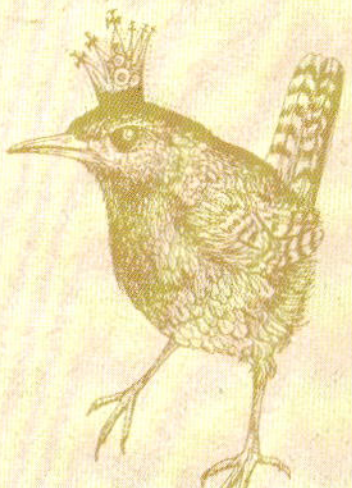

25

The Hedge in Autumn

oil on board

61 x 61 cms   24 x 24 ins

SEAN·JEFFERSON

SOLO EXHIBITIONS

JAN. 1985	'Magic, Mischief & Moonshine', GARDEN GALLERY, New Cross Gate, London.
JAN. 1991	'Mizz-Maze, Embrace of the Shadow', A3 GALLERY, MOSCOW, Paintings, Shadow Boxes and a large maze installation. (covered by Russian media and Reuters)
OCT. 1993	'Whispers Heard Upon Waking', MILL LANE GALLERY with Talisman Fine Art. West Hampstead. Contemporary Symbolist Paintings.
MAY. 1997	'The Fantastic Zoo', JESTER GALLERY, AMSTERDAM, An exhibition based around 10 symbolic animal paintings.
MAY. 2016	CHELSEA ARTS CLUB, Corridor exhibition of small paintings and triptychs.
MAY. 2017	ATLANTIS BOOK SHOP, Exhibition of small esoteric drawings and paintings.
DEC. 2020	DAVID MESSUM FINE ART, St. JAMES'S, First major exhibition since 1997. All new paintings which represent the culmination of 40 years development of a technique for the precise visualisation of the landscapes, flora, fauna and anthropomorphic personages of the inner mind.
DEC. 2023	DAVID MESSUM FINE ART, St. JAMES'S, The Twelve Days of Christmas and Other Works
DEC. 2024	DAVID MESSUM FINE ART, St. JAMES'S, Green Grow the Rushes Oh, A Christmas Carol and Other Works

ISBN 978-1-917240-01-7 Publication No: DIX
Published by David Messum Fine Art

The Studio, Unit 4, Stokenchurch Business Park, Ibstone Rd, HP14 2FE
Tel: 01628 486565 www.messums.com
Photography: Steve Russell, Printed by DLM-Creative